Level 3

Second Edition

Student Text

Authors Matthew Stephens Athena Lester Danielle Nettleton Hope Tolbert	**Designer** Boston Stephens
	Project Coordinator Athena Lester
Teacher Matthew Stephens	**Editor** Athena Lester
Senior Consultant Mary McGee	

417-256-4191
www.essentialsinwriting.com

Printed in the United States of America

LEVEL 3 TABLE OF CONTENTS
UNIT ONE: GRAMMAR

INTRODUCTION

Writing Sentences

PARTS OF SPEECH

Identify Parts of Speech

Common Problems

TOOLS FOR EFFECTIVE COMMUNICATION

Apply Parts of Speech

Apply Sentence Structure

UNIT TWO: COMPOSITION

The Writing Process

Paragraph Practice

Expository Paragraph

Expository Personal Letter

Persuasive Paragraph

Persuasive Personal Letter

Descriptive Paragraph

Imaginative Narrative

Research Project

UNIT ONE: GRAMMAR

Lesson 1 – Introduction to Writing

WRITING

Writing is communicating with written words.

Writing allows us to tell stories, record memories, and inform others.

Learning to write correctly is important for communicating well.

Capitalization, punctuation, spelling, and *spacing* help you communicate with your reader.

Your writing does not need to be perfect the first time. Good writing takes practice.

Writing can be used to:

- explain something to the reader
- describe something
- persuade the reader to agree with you
- tell a story

Lesson 1 – Introduction to Writing

Writing is communicating with written words

Before you begin learning the essentials of writing, it's time to see what you already know.

Read the prompt below and write about it.

Pretend that you have just received a pen pal from a city far away. The pen pal wants to know what you are like. Describe two activities that you like to do.

_____

_____

_____

_____

_____

_____

_____

_____

After you finish your composition, remove this page and place it in a time capsule. Keep it secret; keep it safe. You will not be graded on this composition, so do not worry about making mistakes.

Writing Sentences

✓**Subjects and Predicates**

✓**Types of Sentences**

Lesson 2 – Complete Subjects

The *subject* of a sentence tells the reader who or what the sentence is about. A *complete subject* includes all the words that give information about the subject.

| *complete subject* = An old lady | *complete subject* = Her green scarf |

An old lady *sat on the bench.*   **Her green scarf** *snagged on a nail.*

 Underline the *complete subject* of each sentence.

1. Jackie went to second grade.

2. The little girl wanted a new friend.

3. A boy with a blue hat sat next to her at lunch.

4. His name was Ben.

5. The children played together during recess.

6. Their parents picked them up after school.

7. The new friends waved goodbye to each other.

Complete the sentences with a *subject*.

1. _____ sat on the top shelf.

2. _____ swam across the lake.

3. _____ drank a lot of water after the race.

4. _____ watched two raccoons cross the road.

5

Lesson 2 – Complete Subjects

The *subject* of a sentence tells the reader who or what the sentence is about. A *complete subject* includes all the words that give information about the subject.

A bird with big wings flew across the sky.

| *complete subject* = |
| A bird with big wings |

 Underline the *complete subject* of each sentence in the paragraph.

A big storm blew through a small town. Strong winds destroyed windows and walls! Old buildings fell all over the city! The people in the town were sad after the storm. Then, many men with tools came. The men fixed the broken windows and walls. They built new buildings. The small town thanked the men for their help!

Complete the paragraph by adding *subjects* where they are missing.

_____ liked to ride his bike. _____ is

blue with silver wheels. One day, _____ met a new girl in

his town. _____ said her name was Ella.

_____ also liked to ride her bike. _____

was her favorite place to ride. _____ rode to that place

together on their bikes. _____ became good friends.

6

Lesson 3 – Simple Subjects

A *simple subject* is the main word (noun) of the *complete subject* that tells who or what the sentence is about.

> *simple subject* = lady (the main word in the complete subject)

*An old **lady** sat on the bench.*

> *simple subject* = scarf (the main word in the complete subject)

*Her green **scarf** snagged on a nail.*

 Underline each *simple subject*.

1. Jackie went to second grade.

2. The little girl wanted a new friend.

3. A boy with a blue hat sat next to her at lunch.

4. His name was Ben.

5. The children played together during recess.

6. Their parents picked them up after school.

7. The new friends waved goodbye to each other.

 Complete each sentence with a *simple subject*.

1. The old _____ barked all day.

2. A small _____ fell from the tree.

3. _____ is my sister.

4. _____ saw a frog at the pond.

7

Lesson 3 – Simple Subjects

A *simple subject* is the main word (noun) in the *complete subject* that tells who or what the sentence is about.

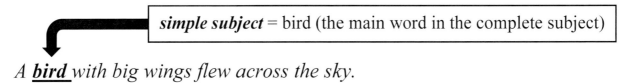

simple subject = bird (the main word in the complete subject)

A ***bird*** *with big wings flew across the sky.*

Underline each *simple subject* in the paragraph below.

A big storm blew through a small town. Strong winds destroyed windows and walls! Old buildings fell all over the city! The people in the town were sad after the storm. Then, many men with tools came. The men fixed the broken windows and walls. They built new buildings. The small town thanked the men for their help!

Complete the paragraph by adding *simple subjects* where they are missing.

_____ likes to cook. His favorite

_____ to make is pasta with sauce. His kind, old

_____ gave him the recipe. _____

made the meal for his family. His _____

loved the meal. _____ is a great cook.

8

Lesson 3 – Simple Subjects

A *simple subject* is the main word (noun) of the *complete subject* that tells who or what the sentence is about.

Seth *claps his hands.*

simple subject = Seth

 Write sentences according to the instructions below. Circle the *simple subject* and underline the *complete subject* of each sentence.

1. Write a sentence about **a dog.**

_____

_____

2. Write a sentence about **rain.**

_____

_____

3. Write a sentence about **a car.**

_____

_____

4. Write a sentence about **tennis.**

_____

_____

Lesson 4 – Complete Predicates

A *predicate* tells what the subject is or does. The *complete predicate* includes the main verb and all other words that complete the verb's meaning.

*An old lady **sat on the bench**.*

complete predicate = sat on the bench

 Underline the *complete predicate* of each sentence.

1. Jackie went to second grade.

2. The little girl wanted a new friend.

3. A boy with a blue hat sat next to her at lunch.

4. His name was Ben.

5. The children played together during recess.

6. Their parents picked them up after school.

7. The new friends waved goodbye to each other.

 Complete each sentence with a *predicate*.

1. A big, black raincloud _____.

2. Mrs. Turner _____.

3. The best store in town _____.

4. Several small dogs _____.

Lesson 4 – Complete Predicates

A *predicate* tells what the subject is or does. The *complete predicate* includes the main verb and all other words that complete the verb's meaning.

A bird with big wings **_flew across the sky_**.

| *complete predicate* = |
| flew across the sky |

 Underline the *complete predicate* of each sentence in the paragraph.

A big storm blew through a small town. Strong winds destroyed windows and walls! Old buildings fell all over the city! The people in the town were sad after the storm. Then, many men with tools came. The men fixed the broken windows and walls. They built new buildings. The small town thanked the men for their help!

Complete the paragraph by adding *predicates* where they are missing.

The Erikson family _____. Their

three children _____. The big

sister _____. The

middle child _____.

Lastly, the little brother _____. The family

_____.

11

Lesson 5 – Simple Predicates

A *simple predicate* is the main word (verb) of the *complete predicate* that tells what the subject is or does.

| *simple predicate* = sat (the main word in the complete predicate) |

*An old lady **sat** on the bench.*

 Underline each *simple predicate*.

1. Jackie went to second grade.

2. The little girl wanted a new friend.

3. A boy with a blue hat sat next to her at lunch.

4. His name was Ben.

5. The children played together during recess.

6. Their parents picked them up after school.

7. The new friends waved goodbye to each other.

 Complete each sentence with a *simple predicate*.

1. The tall stack of books _____ with a loud bang.

2. Theresa _____ the security monitor for thieves.

3. Piles of clean laundry _____ the sofa and the chair.

4. The small green lizard _____ for bugs and other food.

Lesson 5 – Simple Predicates

A *simple predicate* is the main word (verb) of the *complete predicate* that tells what the subject is or does.

> *simple predicate* =
> flew (the main word in the complete predicate)

*A bird with big wings **flew** across the sky.*

 Underline each *simple predicate* in the paragraph below.

A big storm blew through a small town. Strong winds destroyed windows and walls! Old buildings fell all over the city! The people in the town were sad after the storm. Then, many men with tools came. The men fixed the broken windows and walls. They built new buildings. The small town thanked the men for their help!

 Complete the paragraph by adding *simple predicates* where they are missing.

My dad is a math teacher. He _____ a class

full of students. They _____ he is a good

teacher. My dad _____ their homework

every night. My dad _____ teaching.

13

Lesson 5 – Simple Predicates

A *simple predicate* is the main word (verb) of the *complete predicate* that tells what the subject is or does.

Seth **claps** his hands.

| *simple predicate* = |
| claps (the main word in the complete predicate |

 Write sentences according to the instructions below. Circle the *simple predicate* and underline the *complete predicate* of each sentence.

1. Write a sentence about **the sun.**

_____

_____

2. Write a sentence about **a desk.**

_____

_____

3. Write a sentence about **a rat.**

_____

_____

4. Write a sentence about **a path.**

_____

_____

STOP **Complete Assessment 1**

Lesson 6 – Complete and Incomplete Sentences

A **complete sentence** contains both a subject and a predicate. It expresses a complete thought.

| subject | *My friend Tony* *likes cheeseburgers.* | predicate |

An **incomplete sentence** is missing either a subject or a predicate.

 Underline the *complete sentences* and circle the *incomplete sentences* below.

1. Ron built a table.

2. The wolf howled at the moon.

3. Traveling to South Dakota.

4. Frog and Toad are best friends.

5. Unpacked the Christmas lights.

6. The boys with green shoes.

7. French fries are delicious.

8. Six hours on the computer.

9. Eating waffles for breakfast.

10. No chocolate for dogs.

Some of these sentences are incomplete.

Lesson 6 – Complete and Incomplete Sentences

A *complete sentence* contains both a subject and a predicate. It expresses a complete thought. An *incomplete sentence* is missing either a subject or a predicate.

> *add a predicate to make the sentence complete*

A fast car. ➡️ *A fast car <u>zoomed down the road.</u>*

 Correct the *incomplete sentences* on the lines provided. Add either a *subject* or a *predicate*.

1. A giant black dog!

_____

2. Played video games all day.

_____

3. A heavy snowstorm.

_____

4. Watched a movie with his friends.

_____

5. Jogs every morning.

_____

 Underline the *incomplete sentence* in the paragraph below.

Mel has a pet rat. The rat has white fur. It is so small! Rests in a bed. It is a good rat!

 Correct the *incomplete sentence* on the line below.

_____

Lesson 6 – Complete and Incomplete Sentences

A *complete sentence* contains both a subject and a predicate. It expresses a complete thought.

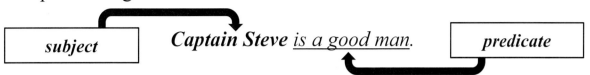

subject   *Captain Steve is a good man.*   predicate

An *incomplete sentence* is missing either a subject or a predicate.

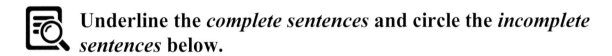 **Underline the *complete sentences* and circle the *incomplete sentences* below.**

1. Went to town.

2. We played all morning.

3. The cats scratched the post.

4. Walks the dog.

5. My mom sang a song at bedtime.

6. Cass swings back and forth.

7. The rain fell.

8. Jon drank the milk.

9. Sat under the willow tree.

10. Told a joke.

Lesson 6 – Complete and Incomplete Sentences

A *complete sentence* contains both a subject and a predicate. It expresses a complete thought. An *incomplete sentence* is missing either a subject or a predicate.

Danced to the music. ➡ ***The man*** *danced to the music.*

add a subject to make the sentence complete

 Correct the *incomplete sentences* on the lines provided. Add either a *subject* or a *predicate*.

1. Melted in the sun.

_____

2. Sent a letter.

_____

3. My sister.

_____

4. The kind doctor.

_____

5. Fell off the swing.

_____

 Underline the *incomplete sentence* in the paragraph below.

Seth is a vet. He helps sick pets. Gives shots. Seth even helps snakes!

Seth is a good vet.

 Correct the *incomplete sentence* on the line below.

_____

Lesson 7 – Types of Sentences and Punctuation Marks

There are four different types of sentences: *declarative*, *interrogative*, *exclamatory*, and *imperative*. Each type of sentence begins with a *capital letter* and must end with the correct *punctuation mark*.

Three types of *punctuation marks* are used to end a sentence: *periods*, *question marks*, and *exclamation points*. Using the correct punctuation tells your reader how a sentence should be read.

Declarative	A *declarative sentence* is a sentence that makes a statement. It always ends with a *period*.
	Example: *The cow munches the grass.*

Interrogative	An *interrogative sentence* is a sentence that asks a question. It always ends with a *question mark*.
	Example: *Are you cold?*

Exclamatory	An exclamatory sentence is a sentence that shows excitement. It always ends with an *exclamation point*.
	Example: *I love my dog!*

Imperative	An imperative sentence is a sentence that gives a command. It can end with a *period* **OR** an *exclamation point*. The subject is always "you," even though it is not written in the sentence.
	Example: *Clean your room.* **OR** *Clean your room!*

Lesson 7 – Types of Sentences and Punctuation Marks

There are four different types of sentences: *declarative*, *interrogative*, *exclamatory*, and *imperative*. Each type of sentence starts with a *capital letter* and must end with the correct *punctuation mark*.

<u>T</u>he dog sniffed the sock<u>.</u> ⬅ declarative

Match the correct punctuation mark to the type of sentence it belongs with.

1. _____ Declarative   A. Question Mark (?)

2. _____ Interrogative   B. Period (.) OR Exclamation Point (!)

3. _____ Exclamatory   C. Period (.)

4. _____ Imperative   D. Exclamation Point (!)

Write whether each sentence is *declarative*, *interrogative*, *exclamatory*, or *imperative*.

1. Where is Mom?   _____

2. Go home right now!   _____

3. This cake is the best!   _____

4. Spot is my dog.   _____

5. Drink the water.   _____

6. Jen is tall.   _____

7. How are you doing today?   _____

8. I am so happy!   _____

Lesson 7 – Types of Sentences and Punctuation Marks

There are four different types of sentences: *declarative*, *interrogative*, *exclamatory*, and *imperative*. Each type of sentence starts with a *capital letter* and must end with the correct *punctuation mark*.

_W_ash the dishes_._ ⟵ | imperative |

The sentences have mistakes in *capitalization* and *punctuation*. Rewrite the sentences correctly.

1. is this your hat

_____

2. come back home

_____

3. the boys swing at the park

_____

4. cal built a tall fort yesterday

_____

5. this is so fun

_____

6. go to bed

_____

Lesson 7 – Types of Sentences and Punctuation Marks

There are four different types of sentences: *declarative*, *interrogative*, *exclamatory*, and *imperative*. Each type of sentence starts with a *capital letter* and must end with the correct *punctuation mark*.

I love you! ⟵ exclamatory

Write sentences according to the instructions below.

1. Write an *imperative sentence* about **a dog.**

_____

_____

2. Write an *exclamatory sentence* about **a bug.**

_____

_____

3. Write an *interrogative sentence* about **a jacket.**

_____

_____

4. Write a *declarative sentence* about **the weather.**

_____

_____

STOP **Complete Assessment 2**

Parts of Speech

√Identify Parts of Speech

√Common Problems

Lesson 8 – Common and Proper Nouns

A ***common noun*** is a word that is any person, place, thing, or idea. A ***proper noun*** is a word that is a specific person, place, thing, or idea, including titles. Proper nouns are capitalized, and common nouns are not capitalized.

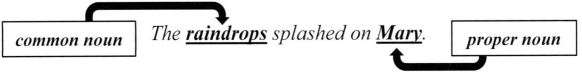

| common noun | The **raindrops** splashed on **Mary**. | proper noun |

 Underline each *common noun*.

1. water bottle	6. Mrs. Robinson	11. spaghetti
2. Jana	7. San Francisco	12. Spot
3. Paris	8. kindness	13. Nobel Prize
4. fence	9. tulips	14. backpack
5. Emmett	10. Arizona	15. mice

 Circle each *proper noun*.

1. Bob Dylan is from the United States.

2. He was born in a city called Duluth.

3. Bob wrote many songs.

4. He went to New York to sing his songs.

5. He won the Medal of Freedom for his songs.

6. Bob Dylan also won the Nobel Prize.

Lesson 8 – Common and Proper Nouns

A *common noun* is a word that is any person, place, thing, or idea. A *proper noun* is a word that is a specific person, place, thing, or idea, including titles. Proper nouns are capitalized, and common nouns are not capitalized.

| proper noun | *__Albany__ is the __city__ where my __uncle__ lives.* | common nouns |

Fill in the blanks with *common nouns*.

1. The _____ went home. (*Person*)

2. The _____ rolled down the hill. (*Thing*)

3. The dog went to the _____. (*Place*)

4. The _____ hits the drums. (*Person*)

Fill in the blanks with *proper nouns*.

1. We went to _____. (*Place*)

2. I have a dog named _____. (*Thing*)

3. _____ went to class. (*Person*)

4. _____ is a big city. (*Place*)

Lesson 8 – Common and Proper Nouns

A *common noun* is a word that is any person, place, thing, or idea. A *proper noun* is a word that is a specific person, place, thing, or idea, including titles. Proper nouns are capitalized, and common nouns are not capitalized.

| common noun | *Kinsby* has a new *dog* named *Chip*. | proper nouns |

 Underline each *common noun* and circle each *proper noun*.

1. Glen walked his dog in France.

2. Kat and Ted played all day.

3. Fuzz is the best cat!

4. Is this map from Canada?

5. Seth plays soccer.

6. Ben called his mom from Texas.

 Underline each *common noun* and circle each *proper noun*.

Beth has a friend named Kim. Kim has long hair. Kim comes from a town in Alaska. Beth has never been to Alaska. Beth is from Maine. Beth writes her friend letters from Maine. Beth would love to visit Kim in Alaska!

Lesson 8 – Common and Proper Nouns

A **_proper noun_** is a word that refers to a specific person, place, thing, or idea, including titles. Proper nouns are capitalized. Capitalize the names of _people, cities, teams, companies, schools,_ and _streets_.

 Rewrite the paragraph below and replace the underlined _common nouns_ with _proper nouns_ that refer to specific people, places, things, or ideas.

A boy moved to _a city_. _A girl_, his sister, liked _the city_, but _the boy_ wished his family had never moved from _another town_. One day, the boy saw _a store_ with a "Help Wanted" sign in the window. He went inside and talked to _a woman_, the owner. She gave _the boy_ a job, and he felt better about being in _the city_.

_____

_____

_____

_____

_____

_____

_____

_____

_____

Lesson 8 – Common and Proper Nouns

A *common noun* is a word that is any person, place, thing, or idea. A *proper noun* is a word that is a specific person, place, thing, or idea, including titles. Proper nouns are capitalized, and common nouns are not capitalized.

| proper nouns | <u>Esther</u> and <u>Eddie</u> like <u>chocolate</u> and <u>cake</u>. | common nouns |

Write sentences according to the instructions below. Use a *proper noun* in each sentence and underline it.

1. Write a sentence about **where you are from.**

_____

_____

2. Write a sentence about **your best friend.**

_____

_____

3. Write a sentence about **a sibling.**

_____

_____

4. Write a sentence about **a pet.**

_____

_____

Lesson 9 – Singular and Plural Nouns

A *singular noun* refers to <u>one</u> person, place, thing, or idea. A *plural noun* refers to <u>more than one</u> person, place, thing, or idea. Most words are made plural by adding *-s*.

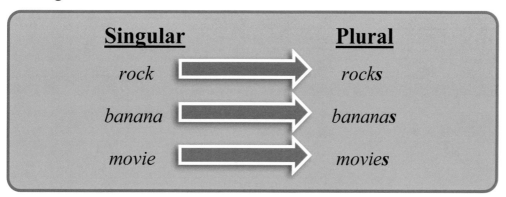

Words that end with the letters *-ch, -sh, -s, -x*, and *-z* are made plural by adding *-es*.

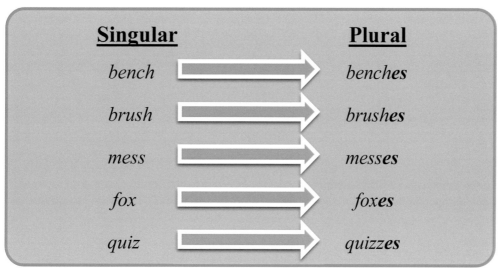

Some nouns have *irregular* plural forms. When these nouns become plural, their spelling completely changes.

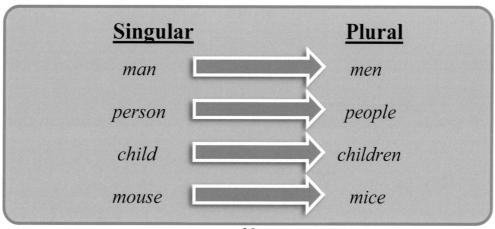

Lesson 9 – Singular and Plural Nouns

A *singular noun* refers to <u>one</u> person, place, thing, or idea. A *plural noun* refers to <u>more than one</u> person, place, thing, or idea.

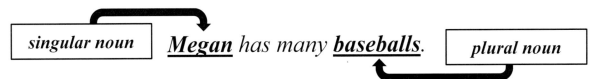

| singular noun | *__Megan__ has many **baseballs**.* | plural noun |

 Underline the *singular nouns* and circle the *plural nouns* below.

1. Kelly jumped over the lines.

2. The woman sang songs.

3. The books fell from the shelf.

4. Jim writes with the pen.

5. The cats sleep on the steps.

6. Can the girls swim in the lake?

7. Jenna plays the drums.

8. Birds make the best pets!

9. Cass takes care of the horses.

10. The cups are full.

Lesson 9 – Singular and Plural Nouns

A *singular noun* refers to <u>one</u> person, place, thing, or idea. A *plural noun* refers to <u>more than one</u> person, place, thing, or idea.

| singular nouns |

My **<u>grandpa</u>** has one **<u>bunny</u>** and three **<u>dogs</u>**. | plural noun |

Fill in the blank with the *plural* of the indicated noun.

1. The _____ sit on the fence. (*bird*)

2. Hal made blue clay _____. (*cup*)

3. My cat is stuck in the _____! (*branch*)

4. A dad got gifts for his _____. (*girl*)

5. The _____ ring bells. (*church*)

6. My _____ are cold! (*hand*)

Write the *plural* form of each noun in the boxes below.

Singular	Plural	Singular	Plural
forest		person	
boss		coat	
six		dish	
photo		trench	
river		table	

31

Lesson 9 – Singular and Plural Nouns

A *singular noun* refers to <u>one</u> person, place, thing, or idea. A *plural noun* refers to <u>more than one</u> person, place, thing, or idea.

| singular noun |
| plural noun |

*The old <u>**rug**</u> was covered with colorful <u>**presents**</u>.*

 Underline the *singular nouns* and circle the *plural nouns* in the paragraph below.

Emilio has two birds. The birds were presents from his parents. One bird is Chipper. The other bird is Airplane. Chipper has bright feathers, and Airplane has a long beak. Emilio feeds his birds in little bowls. The birds drink water from bottles. Emilio takes care of Chipper and Airplane and loves his birds very much.

Write the *plural* form of each noun in the boxes below.

Singular	Plural	Singular	Plural
arm		flower	
wish		woman	
actor		beach	
class		kitten	
stream		block	

Lesson 9 – Singular and Plural Nouns

A *singular noun* refers to <u>one</u> person, place, thing, or idea. A *plural noun* refers to <u>more than one</u> person, place, thing, or idea.

 The paragraph below contains errors in plural spellings of nouns. Rewrite the paragraph below, spelling each of the plural nouns correctly.

I play with many <u>kides</u> in my town. We play <u>gamess</u> like jump rope and tag. Beth is the best tagger! She once tagged two <u>girles</u> at the same time! We also draw <u>boxs</u> on the sidewalk and play hopscotch. After playing, we like to rest on the <u>benchs</u> at the park. Playing with <u>friendes</u> is fun!

Lesson 9 – Singular and Plural Nouns

A *singular noun* refers to one person, place, thing, or idea. A *plural noun* refers to more than one person, place, thing, or idea.

| plural noun | My <u>sisters</u> went to a <u>***party***</u> in <u>***Springfield***</u>. | singular nouns |

Write sentences according to the instructions below. Use a *plural noun* in each sentence and underline it.

1. Write a sentence about **a type of dog.**

_____

_____

2. Write a sentence about **a summer activity.**

_____

_____

3. Write a sentence about **a chore you do.**

_____

_____

4. Write a sentence about **your birthday.**

_____

_____

STOP   **Complete Assessment 3**

Lesson 10 – Pronouns and Antecedents

A ***pronoun*** is a word that can be used in place of a noun. The word that the pronoun replaces is called an ***antecedent***.

List of Pronouns					
I	me	my	you	your	he
him	his	she	her	it	its
they	them	their	we	us	our

Tyrone *made a cake.* ***He*** *made a cake.*

 Underline the *pronouns*.

1. Jim sang a song. It was so pretty!

2. Kelly jumped on the bed. She was happy.

3. Harry had a scarf. Les gave it to him.

4. Jess tells us about her bunny. We think it is cute!

5. Liv spilled the tea on me. I was upset.

 Circle the *antecedents*.

1. Ken drove home. He parked the car.

2. Elle came to the party. She wore a red dress.

3. The dog jumped on my lap. It fell asleep.

4. Jen and Ness play the drums. They are so talented!

5. Al and I went to the store. We got bread.

Lesson 10 – Pronouns and Antecedents

A *pronoun* is a word that can be used in place of a noun. The word that the pronoun replaces is called an *antecedent*.

	List of Pronouns				
I	me	my	you	your	he
him	his	she	her	it	its
they	them	their	we	us	our

Jess played the drums. ➡ *She* played the drums.

Rewrite the sentences and replace the underlined nouns with the correct *pronouns*.

1. Gal's best friend is <u>Gal's</u> sister.

_____

2. Hal worked on <u>Hal's</u> project all night.

_____

3. Mrs. Tally told Jessica that <u>Jessica</u> was pretty.

_____

4. Dev and Caleb saved <u>Dev and Caleb's</u> money.

_____

5. Bri and I want Lindsey to join <u>Bri and me</u>.

_____

6. I have a book, and I took <u>the book</u> to the park.

_____

Lesson 10 – Pronouns and Antecedents

A ***pronoun*** is a word that can be used in place of a noun. The word that the pronoun replaces is called an ***antecedent***.

List of Pronouns					
I	me	my	you	your	he
him	his	she	her	it	its
they	them	their	we	us	our

Cal and I *sang for* ***our family***. ➡ ***We*** *sang for* ***them***.

 Underline the *pronouns* in the paragraph below.

Callie and John are siblings. They are my friends, and they both play the piano. Callie likes to play rag music. She plays so fast! John likes to play songs by Brahms. His music is pretty. Callie and John play songs for us. We love to hear them play!

 Circle the *antecedents* in the paragraph below.

Micah has two little bunnies. They are named Wes and Mollie, and they are his pets. Wes has a pink nose. He wiggles it. Mollie has a fuzzy white tail. She is so cute! They live in a small hutch. It keeps Wes and Mollie safe. Micah loves his pet bunnies so much!

Lesson 10 – Pronouns and Antecedents

A *pronoun* is a word that can be used in place of a noun. The word that the pronoun replaces is called an ***antecedent***.

<u>Elle</u> held the <u>cat</u>. ➡ *<u>She</u> held <u>it</u>.*

Read the paragraph below. Rewrite the paragraph, replacing the underlined nouns with the correct *pronouns*.

Beth has a bell. Grandma gave <u>the bell</u> to <u>Beth</u>. The bell is gold.

Beth rings <u>the bell</u> every afternoon. <u>Beth</u> loves the bell.

_____

_____

_____

_____

_____

_____

_____

Lesson 10 – Pronouns and Antecedents

A ***pronoun*** is a word that can be used in place of a noun. The word that the pronoun replaces is called an ***antecedent***.

 Read the paragraph below.

Easton and Jay played basketball together. Easton and Jay practiced every day together with the team, and Easton and Jay also practiced alone. Easton and Jay wanted to do Easton and Jay's very best. Easton and Jay's coach noticed Easton and Jay's hard work. Easton and Jay's coach made Easton and Jay starters for the big game. Easton and Jay were so excited! Easton and Jay knew Easton and Jay's extra practice had paid off.

Which is missing? 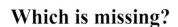 | pronouns | antecedents

 Read the paragraph again below.

They played basketball together. They practiced every day together with the team, and they also practiced alone. They wanted to do their very best. Their coach noticed their hard work. Their coach made them starters for the big game. They were so excited! They knew their extra practice had paid off.

Which is missing? | pronouns | antecedents

Lesson 10 – Pronouns and Antecedents

A *pronoun* is a word that can be used in place of a noun. The word that the pronoun replaces is called an *antecedent*.

Rewrite the paragraph from the previous page, using both *antecedents* and *pronouns* correctly.

_____

_____

_____

_____

_____

_____

_____

_____

_____

_____

_____

Lesson 10 – Pronouns and Antecedents

A *pronoun* is a word that can be used in place of a noun. The word that the pronoun replaces is called an *antecedent*.

*Lin and Beth have a pool. **Lin and Beth** like to swim.*

*Lin and Beth have a pool. **They** like to swim.*

Write sentences according to the instructions below. Underline each *pronoun* you use and circle the *antecedents*.

1. Write two sentences about **your pet.** Use a pronoun in the second sentence.

_____

_____

_____

_____

2. Write two sentences about **your house.** Use a pronoun in the second sentence.

_____

_____

_____

_____

STOP **Complete Assessment 4**

Lesson 11 – Singular Possessive Nouns

A *possessive noun* shows ownership or relationship between two nouns. To make a *singular noun* show possession, add *'s* to the end.

possessive noun

The bike of the boy...... ➡ *The **boy** 's bike ......*

Use *possessive nouns* to shorten the phrases.

1. the box of the crayon _____

2. the price of the toy _____

3. the wheel of the truck _____

4. the page of the book _____

5. the collar of the dress _____

6. the bed of the cat _____

7. the light of the lamp _____

8. the shape of the cloud _____

9. the hair of the woman _____

10. the slobber of the dog _____

Lesson 11 – Singular Possessive Nouns

A *possessive noun* shows ownership or relationship between two nouns. To make a *singular noun* show possession, add *'s* to the end.

I rode the skateboard. The skateboard belonged to my friend.

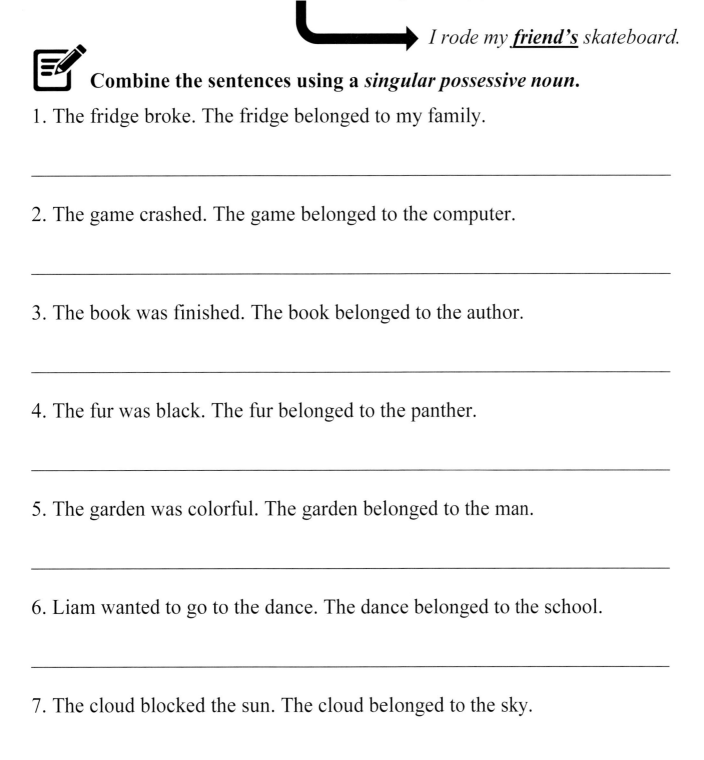

*I rode my **friend's** skateboard.*

Combine the sentences using a *singular possessive noun*.

1. The fridge broke. The fridge belonged to my family.

_____

2. The game crashed. The game belonged to the computer.

_____

3. The book was finished. The book belonged to the author.

_____

4. The fur was black. The fur belonged to the panther.

_____

5. The garden was colorful. The garden belonged to the man.

_____

6. Liam wanted to go to the dance. The dance belonged to the school.

_____

7. The cloud blocked the sun. The cloud belonged to the sky.

_____

Lesson 12 – Plural Possessive Nouns

A *possessive noun* shows ownership or relationship between two nouns. To make a *plural noun* that ends in -s possessive, add only an *apostrophe* (') to the end.

plural possessive noun

The animals of the farmers...... ➡ *The __farmers'__ animals ......*

Use *possessive nouns* to shorten the phrases.

1. the homes of the families _____

2. the hisses of the cats _____

3. the colors of the leaves _____

4. the pictures of the books _____

5. the meeting of the leaders _____

6. the secret of the caves _____

7. the speed of the horses _____

8. the boats of the rivers _____

9. the smell of the clothes _____

10. the shape of the numbers _____

Lesson 12 – Plural Possessive Nouns

A *possessive noun* shows ownership or relationship between two nouns. To make a *plural noun* that ends in *-s* possessive, add only an *apostrophe* (') to the end.

The tires were flat. The tires belong to the trucks.

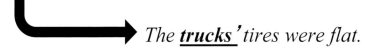

*The **trucks** ' tires were flat.*

 Combine the sentences using a *plural possessive noun*.

1. The powers were amazing. The powers belonged to the heroes.

_____

2. The light twinkled in the sky. The light belonged to the stars.

_____

3. The bread smelled delicious. The bread belonged to the bakers.

_____

4. The cubs searched for blueberries. The cubs belonged to the bears.

_____

5. The fish leaped out of the water. The fish belonged to the rivers.

_____

6. The voices drifted through the air. The voices belonged to the singers.

_____

7. The leaves dropped to the ground. The leaves belonged to the trees.

_____

Lesson 13 – More Plural Possessive Nouns

A *possessive noun* shows ownership or relationship between two nouns. To make a *plural noun* that does <u>not</u> end in *-s* possessive, add *'s* to the end.

plural possessive noun

The toys of the children...... ➡️ *The **children's** toys ......*

✏️ **Use *possessive nouns* to shorten these phrases.**

1. the beaks of the geese _____

2. the antlers of the deer _____

3. the carts of the oxen _____

4. the jobs of the women _____

5. the edges of the teeth _____

6. the homes of the moose _____

7. the legs of the shrimp _____

8. the ears of the sheep _____

9. the whiskers of the mice _____

10. the shouts of the people _____

Lesson 13 – More Plural Possessive Nouns

A *possessive noun* shows ownership or relationship between two nouns. To make a *plural noun* that does <u>not</u> end in *-s* possessive, add *'s* to the end.

The edges were sharp. The edges belonged to the teeth.

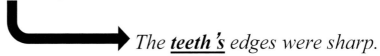 *The **<u>teeth's</u>** edges were sharp.*

 Combine the sentences using a *plural possessive noun*.

1. The sirens were loud. The sirens belonged to the policemen.

_____

2. The tank was dirty. The tank belonged to the fish.

_____

3. The meadow was sunny. The meadow belonged to the deer.

_____

4. The concert was popular. The concert belonged to the women.

_____

5. The feathers were everywhere. The feathers belonged to the geese.

_____

6. The wool was soft. The wool belonged to the sheep.

_____

7. The pets ran loose. The pets belonged to the children.

_____

Lesson 13 – More Plural Possessive Nouns

A *possessive noun* shows ownership or relationship between two nouns.

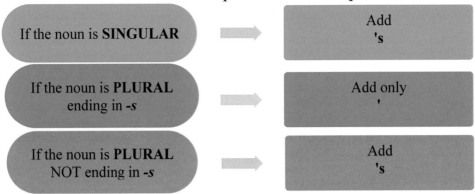

If the noun is **SINGULAR**	Add 's
If the noun is **PLURAL** ending in -s	Add only '
If the noun is **PLURAL** NOT ending in -s	Add 's

 Write sentences according to the instructions below. Use a *possessive noun* in each sentence and underline it.

1. Write a sentence about **the pet of your friend**.

_____

_____

2. Write a sentence about **the car of your family**.

_____

_____

3. Write a sentence about **a toy that belongs to a sibling**.

_____

_____

4. Write a sentence about **the fur of a kitten**.

_____

_____

STOP **Complete Assessment 5**

Lesson 14 – Adjectives

An **adjective** changes or describes a noun in a sentence. **Adjectives** are tools authors use to help readers see, smell, taste, hear, feel, and experience what is described.

adjective

*The **spicy** chips burned my mouth!*

Underline the *adjectives* in the sentences.

1. The quick runner won the race!

2. The noisy dogs barked during the night.

Adjectives add greater detail to nouns and help the reader see a better picture in their mind.

3. My dad carved the giant turkey.

4. Heavy rain pelted us as we ran for cover.

5. Flowery dresses filled the window.

6. We looked up at the fluffy clouds.

7. Sleepy students struggled to keep their eyes open.

8. Yellow tulips waved in the gentle wind.

9. Bright lamps covered the room in light.

10. The red fox slept in the tall grass.

11. Huge waves crashed in the blue sea!

12. Soft snow fell from the sky.

Lesson 14 – Adjectives

An *adjective* changes or describes a noun in a sentence. *Adjectives* are tools authors use to help readers see, smell, taste, hear, feel, and experience what is described.

*My grandma made a cake that tastes **amazing**!* | adjective |

 Complete each sentence with an *adjective*.

NOTE: Avoid writing verbs on the lines.

Incorrect: The children are <u>playing</u>.

Correct: The children are <u>upset</u>.

1. The roads are _____.

2. My friends are _____.

3. _____ berries grow on the bushes in the forest.

4. The schoolhouse is _____.

5. The _____ building is the library.

6. I am _____.

7. The concert played _____ music.

8. You are _____.

9. A(n) _____ dog suddenly blocked our path.

10. My mother is a(n) _____ person.

Lesson 14 – Adjectives

An *adjective* changes or describes a noun in a sentence. *Adjectives* are tools authors use to help readers see, smell, taste, hear, feel, and experience what is described.

*A girl found a **large** wardrobe in the **extra** room.*

*The lamppost in the forest was **strange** but **lovely**.*

 Underline the *adjectives* in the paragraph below.

Emily has a little bird. The little bird is yellow. It sings pretty songs, and it says funny things. Emily lets the bird fly around her big bedroom. It sleeps in a tiny, purple cage. The little bird is Emily's favorite pet.

 Underline the *adjectives* in the paragraph below.

Seth loves to build. He makes strong wooden tables and tall desks. Seth built a red shelf a friend named Jennifer. She said it was a wonderful gift! Seth is a great builder.

Lesson 14 – Adjectives

An *adjective* changes or describes a noun in a sentence. *Adjectives* are tools authors use to help readers see, smell, taste, hear, feel, and experience what is described.

 Rewrite the paragraph below. Add at least one *adjective* to each sentence.

I ate my lunch at a table. I saw a girl across the room. She wore a hat and boots. The girl was eating a sandwich by herself. Finally, I left my table and crossed the room to her. I asked her if she wanted to sit at my table. The girl said yes. Now, we are friends.

_____

_____

_____

_____

_____

_____

_____

_____

Lesson 14 – Adjectives

An *adjective* changes or describes a noun in a sentence. *Adjectives* are tools authors use to help readers see, smell, taste, hear, feel, and experience what is described.

adjectives

*The **creamy** stew had **tender** beef and **tasty** veggies.*

Write sentences according to the instructions below. Use an *adjective* in each sentence and underline it.

1. Write a sentence about **breakfast.** What is breakfast like?

_____

_____

2. Write a sentence about **the mall.** What is the mall like?

_____

_____

3. Write a sentence about **rain.** What is the rain like?

_____

_____

4. Write a sentence about **a rat.** What is the rat like?

_____

STOP **Complete Assessment 6**

Lesson 15 – Action Verbs

An *action verb* tells what the subject does. Action verbs are found in the predicate.

| action verb |

*My little brother **raced** to the finish line!*

 Circle each *action verb*.

1. A rat lived in Paris.

2. He loved the food in the city.

3. He dreamed of kitchens and restaurants.

4. His father disliked this dream.

5. Chefs worked in kitchens, not rats.

6. A human chef helped the rat.

7. The rat inspired the human.

8. Together, they cooked amazing food.

9. The human chef also found love!

10. The rat and human made a good team.

 Circle the *action verb* in each row of words.

1.	leash	walk	fur	path
2.	desk	marker	scribble	workbook
3.	knife	glass	chew	placemat
4.	phone	purse	number	call
5.	watch	game	glasses	hat
6.	music	keys	play	cord

54

Lesson 15 – Action Verbs

An *action verb* tells what the subject does. Action verbs are found in the predicate.

action verb

A butterfly __fluttered__ by the car window.

Complete each sentence with an *action verb*.

1. Cats and dogs _____ from their food bowls.

2. The group of students _____ into the bus.

3. Dark, thick clouds _____ the sun.

4. The children _____ doorbells on Halloween.

5. Lila _____ toward the finish line.

6. The doctor _____ down the hall toward the patient.

7. Sarah and Caleb _____ water after playing outside.

8. My dad _____ five fish yesterday.

9. Chefs _____ desserts of all kinds at the restaurant.

Lesson 15 – Action Verbs

An *action verb* tells what the subject does. Action verbs are found in the predicate.

action verb

*Several cereal boxes **tumbled** off the supermarket shelf.*

 Circle each *action verb* in the paragraph below.

Salem plays on a soccer team. He practices after class every day.

He and his friend Zak kick the ball back and forth. Salem scores goals at the

games. Zak scores goals too! Everyone cheers in the stands. Their team lifts

them in the air. The team won the soccer match!

 Complete the paragraph with *action verbs*.

Jen and Max _____ at a coffee shop.

Jen was _____ a book when Max came

up and _____ to

her. Max _____ Jen on a date. Years

later, Jen and Max _____ each other.

They _____ in a little house by the sea.

Lesson 15 – Action Verbs

An *action verb* tells what the subject does. Action verbs are found in the predicate.

action verb

*The policeman **drove** his police car.*

Write sentences according to the instructions below. Underline the *action verb* in each sentence.

1. Write a sentence about **what a tiger does.**

_____

_____

2. Write a sentence about **what a fireman does**.

_____

_____

3. Write a sentence about **what a bird does**.

_____

_____

4. Write a sentence about **what a doctor does**.

_____

_____

Lesson 16 – Present, Past, and Future Tense Action Verbs

An *action verb* tells what the subject does.

Action verbs that describe something happening right now are in the *present tense*. The action is happening in the present—right now!

*Jack **strums** the guitar.*

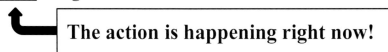

The action is happening right now!

Most verbs in the *present tense* end with an *-s.*

calls	turns	laughs	dances	hugs

Verbs can also be in the *past tense*. They describe something that happened in the past. The action already happened!

*Jack **strummed** the guitar.*

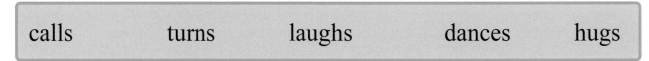

The action is not happening right now. The action happened in the past.

Most verbs in the past tense end with *-ed.*

called	turned	laughed	danced	hugged

Verbs can also be in the *future tense*. They describe something that happens in the future. The action will happen later!

*Jack **will strum** the guitar.*

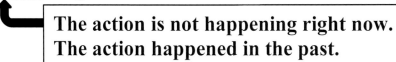

The action has not happened yet. The action will happen in the future.

Future tense action verbs are two words: **"will + *verb*."**

will call	will turn	will laugh	will dance	will hug

Lesson 16 – Present, Past, and Future Tense Action Verbs

Action verbs that describe something happening right now are in the *present tense*. Action verbs that describe something that already happened are in the *past tense*. Action verbs that describe something that will happen are in the *future tense*.

*Hal **plays** soccer.*　　*Hal **played** soccer.*　　*Hall **will play** soccer.*

present tense　　　past tense　　　future tense

Write whether the underlined verbs are in the *present tense*, the *past tense*, or the *future tense*.

Present *OR* Past *OR* Future ?

1. Cass <u>peeled</u> the orange slowly. _____

2. The panda <u>sleeps</u> all night. _____

3. We <u>will go</u> to the store tomorrow. _____

4. Sam often <u>talks</u> loudly. _____

5. The bulky cow <u>chews</u> the grass. _____

6. Mom <u>will send</u> the letter. _____

7. The writer <u>typed</u> on the computer. _____

8. My sister <u>cries</u> after the movie. _____

9. I <u>will try</u> my best at the game! _____

10. The puppy <u>sniffed</u> my shoes. _____

Lesson 16 – Present, Past, and Future Tense Action Verbs

Action verbs that describe something happening right now are in the *present tense*. Action verbs that describe something that already happened are in the *past tense*. Action verbs that describe something that will happen are in the *future tense*.

Dan **scrubs** *the floor.*   Dan **scrubbed** *the floor.*   Dan **will scrub** *the floor.*

| present tense | | past tense | | future tense |

Rewrite the sentences and change the *present tense* action verbs to the tense indicated.

1. The poodle <u>barks</u> at the man.

Past: _____

2. Water <u>spills</u> from the glass.

Future: _____

3. Mia <u>plays</u> the piano.

Past: _____

4. Trees <u>sway</u> in the wind.

Future: _____

5. The picture frame <u>shatters</u>.

Past: _____

6. The boy <u>talks</u> to his teacher.

Future: _____

Lesson 16 – Present, Past, and Future Tense Action Verbs

Action verbs that describe something happening right now are in the *present tense*. Action verbs that describe something that already happened are in the *past tense*. Action verbs that describe something that will happen are in the *future tense*.

Beck **calls** her mom.   Beck **called** her mom.   Beck **will call** her mom.

| present tense | | past tense | | future tense |

Write whether the underlined verbs are in the *present tense*, the *past tense*, or the *future tense*.

Present *OR* Past *OR* Future ?

1. The fox <u>will dig</u> a den.   _____

2. She <u>tended</u> the sheep.   _____

3. Bees <u>buzz</u> in the garden.   _____

4. The boy <u>strummed</u> the instrument.   _____

5. Tad <u>marches</u> to the beat.   _____

6. Mark <u>will give</u> a gift to his mom.   _____

7. Kites <u>soar</u> in the sky.   _____

8. My sister <u>will like</u> the movie.   _____

9. The toy <u>spins</u> around like a top.   _____

10. The waitress <u>dropped</u> the tray.   _____

Lesson 16 – Present, Past, and Future Tense Action Verbs

Action verbs that describe something happening right now are in the *present tense*. Action verbs that describe something that already happened are in the *past tense*. Action verbs that describe something that will happen are in the *future tense*.

He **parks** the car.   He **parked** the car.   He **will park** the car.

↱ *present tense*   ↱ *past tense*   ↱ *future tense*

Rewrite the sentences and change the *present tense* action verbs to the tense indicated.

1. Sam <u>steams</u> a cup of milk.

Past: _____

2. The sandcastle <u>crumbles</u>.

Future: _____

3. A snail <u>moves</u> slowly.

Past: _____

4. Wolves <u>howl</u> at the moon.

Future: _____

5. Ezra <u>tosses</u> the ball to Jerry.

Past: _____

6. I <u>make</u> a cake for the party.

Future: _____

Lesson 17 – Irregular Action Verbs

Many common verbs are *irregular*. They do not follow the same tense pattern as other verbs. You need to know the *present, past,* and *future tenses* of certain *irregular verbs*.

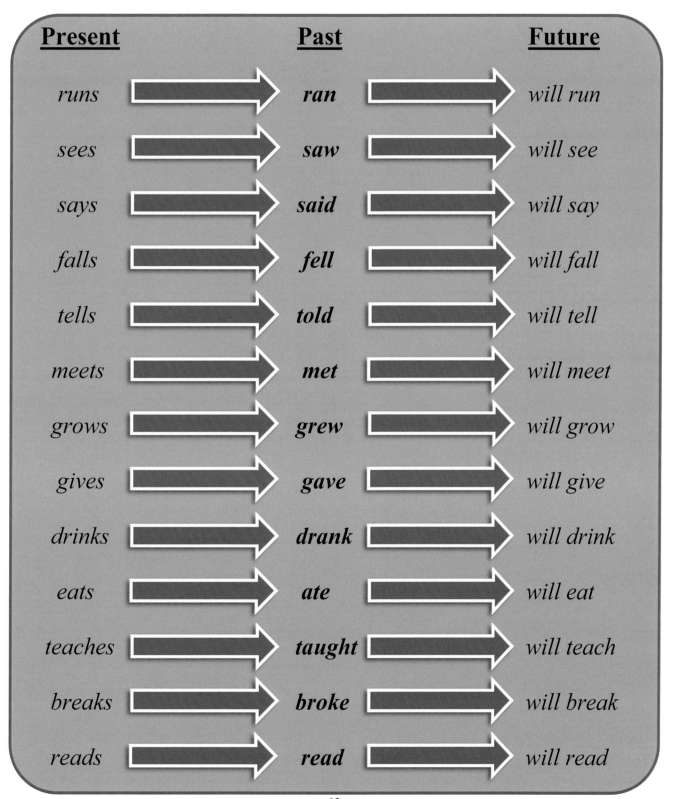

Present	Past	Future
runs	ran	will run
sees	saw	will see
says	said	will say
falls	fell	will fall
tells	told	will tell
meets	met	will meet
grows	grew	will grow
gives	gave	will give
drinks	drank	will drink
eats	ate	will eat
teaches	taught	will teach
breaks	broke	will break
reads	read	will read

Lesson 17 – Irregular Action Verbs

Many common verbs are *irregular*. They do not follow the same tense pattern as other verbs. You need to know the *present, past,* and *future tenses* of certain *irregular verbs*.

 Rewrite the sentences and change the *present tense* verbs to *past tense* verbs.

1. The rat <u>runs</u> into the box.

_____

2. Lilies <u>grow</u> in the summer.

_____

3. The swimmer <u>drinks</u> water from a bottle.

_____

4. The lioness <u>eats</u> antelope for dinner.

_____

5. Mrs. Zusak <u>teaches</u> piano lessons.

_____

6. My older sister <u>reads</u> so many books!

_____

7. In the autumn, leaves <u>fall</u> to the ground.

_____

8. Dad <u>says</u> I have to clean the car.

_____

Lesson 17 – Irregular Action Verbs

Many common verbs are *irregular*. They do not follow the same tense pattern as other verbs. You need to know the *present, past,* and *future tenses* of certain *irregular verbs*.

 Write sentences according to the instructions below. Underline the *action verb* **in each sentence. You can use** *regular* **or** *irregular* **action verbs**

1. Write a sentence about **a horse.** Use a *present tense* verb.

_____

_____

2. Write a sentence about **your dad.** Use a *past tense* verb.

_____

_____

3. Write a sentence about **two dogs.** Use a *future tense* verb.

_____

_____

4. Write a sentence about **a tree.** Use a *past tense* verb.

_____

_____

5. Write a sentence about **yourself.** Use a *future tense* verb.

_____

_____

Lesson 18– Linking Verbs

A *linking verb* links the subject to a word or phrase in the predicate. A *linking verb* helps describe a subject rather than telling what the subject does.

*Dolphins **are** sea animals.* | linking verb |

 Underline each *linking verb*.

| **Common Linking Verbs** |
| am, is, are, was, were |

1. I am tired today.

2. Jax and Luna were sad because of the rain.

3. The fox was red and white.

4. Andrea is a great singer!

5. We were excited for the play.

6. Hamsters are small rodents.

7. Is this your house?

 Circle each *linking verb*. Cross out words that are <u>not</u> *linking verbs*.

is	live	hold	begin	were	turn
run	are	have	drink	look	ate
sail	beg	am	show	was	make

66

Lesson 18 – Linking Verbs

A *linking verb* links the subject to a word or phrase in the predicate. A *linking verb* helps describe a subject rather than telling what the subject does.

linking verb

Robin and Barney __were__ the very best friends.

 Complete each sentence with a *linking verb*.

Common Linking Verbs

am, is, are, was, were

1. My puppy _____ so tiny!

2. Kendra and Sam _____ best friends.

3. I _____ tired after a long day.

4. Mom said she _____ alone yesterday.

5. You _____ so funny at the talent show!

6. The art at the museum _____ beautiful.

7. I _____ tall as a child.

8. Lex and Tris _____ happy I was home.

9. _____ this your hat?

10. I _____ so excited for my trip!

Lesson 18 – Linking Verbs

A *linking verb* links the subject to a word or phrase in the predicate. A *linking verb* helps describe a subject rather than telling what the subject does.

The house at the end of the lane is old and spooky. | linking verb |

 Underline each *linking verb* in the paragraph below.

| **Common Linking Verbs** |
| am, is, are, was, were |

My mom is a vet. She helps dogs and cats when they are sick.

She was in school for a very long time. My family and I were so

happy for her when she finished! Now, she has her own clinic. We

are all so proud of her!

Complete each sentence with a *linking verb* in the paragraph below.

Johnny _____ my older brother. He _____

tall and slim. His eyes_____ brown, and his hair

_____ blonde. Johnny _____ also a

great swimmer! He and I _____ best friends. I

_____ so happy he _____ my brother.

Lesson 19 – Present, Past, and Future Tense Linking Verbs

A *linking verb* is a verb that connects the subject to a word or phrase in the predicate. It helps describe a subject instead of telling what the subject does.

Just like action verbs, linking verbs that describe what the subject is like right now are in the *present tense*. Linking verbs that describe what the subject was like in the past are in the *past tense*. Lastly, linking verbs that describe what a subject will be like in the future are in the *future tense*.

These linking verbs are *irregular verbs*. Because we use them so much, it is important to know the tenses of the common linking verbs.

Present	**Past**	**Future**
I **_am_** a doctor.	I **_was_** a doctor.	I **_will be_** a doctor.
You **_are_** tired.	You **_were_** tired.	You **_will be_** tired.
It **_is_** hot today.	It **_was_** hot today.	It **_will be_** hot today.
They **_are_** tasty.	They **_were_** tasty.	They **_will be_** tasty.

As you can see, it will be easy to remember the future tense of all the common linking verbs. They are exactly the same!

Lesson 19 – Present, Past, and Future Tense Linking Verbs

Just like action verbs, linking verbs that describe what the subject is like right now are in the *present tense*. Linking verbs that describe what the subject was like in the past are in the *past tense*. Lastly, linking verbs that describe what a subject will be like in the future are in the *future tense*.

*Jon **is** a farmer.*   *Jon **was** farmer*   *Jon **will be** a farmer.*

present tense   *past tense*   *future tense*

Write whether the underlined verbs are in the *present tense*, the *past tense*, or the *future tense*.

Present *OR* Past *OR* Future ?

1. I <u>am</u> sorry for being late. _____

2. Cass <u>was</u> upset with me. _____

3. This year <u>will be</u> great! _____

4. June <u>is</u> shorter than Kelly. _____

5. I <u>will be</u> a scientist one day _____

6. You <u>are</u> so funny! _____

7. I <u>was</u> too excited to sleep. _____

8. The ducks <u>are</u> swimming. _____

9. Dan and Phil <u>will be</u> at my party! _____

10. They <u>were</u> at the play. _____

Lesson 19 – Present, Past, and Future Tense Linking Verbs

Just like action verbs, linking verbs that describe what the subject is like right now are in the *present tense*. Linking verbs that describe what the subject was like in the past are in the *past tense*. Lastly, linking verbs that describe what a subject will be like in the future are in the *future tense*.

*Liz and Jo **are** dancers.   Liz and Jo **were** dancers.   Liz and Jo **will be** dancers.*

present tense   past tense   future tense

Rewrite the sentences and change the *present tense* linking verbs to the tense indicated.

1. His hair is brown.

Past: _____

2. All the songs are pretty.

Future: _____

3. I am too cold to go outside.

Past: _____

4. The color of the frosting is blue.

Future: _____

5. Cars are big and fast.

Past: _____

6. I am kind and friendly.

Future: _____

Lesson 19 – Present, Past, and Future Tense Linking Verbs

Just like action verbs, linking verbs that describe what the subject is like right now are in the *present tense*. Linking verbs that describe what the subject was like in the past are in the *past tense*. Lastly, linking verbs that describe what a subject will be like in the future are in the *future tense*.

 Write sentences according to the instructions below. Use a *linking verb* in each sentence and underline it.

1. Write a sentence about **your home.** Use a *present tense* linking verb.

_____

_____

2. Write a sentence about **a frog.** Use a *past tense* linking verb.

_____

_____

3. Write a sentence about **a girl named Jess.** Use a *future tense* linking verb.

_____

_____

4. Write a sentence about **a pillow.** Use a *past tense* linking verb.

_____

_____

5. Write a sentence about **yourself.** Use a *future tense* linking verb.

_____

_____

STOP **Complete Assessment 7**

Lesson 20 – Adverbs That Modify Verbs

An **adverb** changes a verb. A verb tells *what* the subject is doing. An **adverb** tells *how* the subject is doing that action.

Just like adjectives describe nouns, **adverbs** describe verbs. Most **adverbs** end with *-ly*. Usually, an **adverb** is formed by adding *-ly* to the end of an adjective.

Adjectives	Adverbs
gentle	gent**ly**
sad	sad**ly**
quick	quick**ly**
hopeful	hopeful**ly**

However, some **adverbs** do not end in *-ly*. Words like *well, always, almost, now,* and *later* are common **adverbs** that do not end in *-ly*.

Adverbs may come before the verb.

*The cat **carefully** walked on the fence*

An **adverb** may also come after the verb.

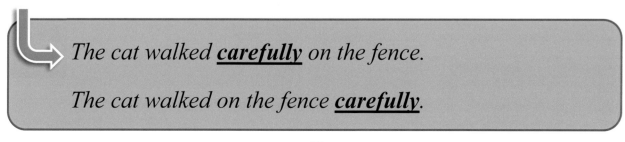

*The cat walked **carefully** on the fence.*

*The cat walked on the fence **carefully**.*

Lesson 20 – Adverbs That Modify Verbs

An *adverb* changes a verb. A verb tells *what* the subject is doing. An *adverb* tells *how* the subject is doing that action. Most *adverbs* end with *-ly*.

 Underline each *adverb* in the sentences.

1. The fox quickly runs to his den.

2. My uncle snores loudly.

3. Sal clumsily dropped the dishes.

4. The door slammed suddenly.

5. Susan and Todd happily made grilled cheese sandwiches.

6. Snow softly drifts to the ground.

7. The girl calmly reads all afternoon.

8. The sun brightly shines on the grass.

9. Waves crashed powerfully in the sea.

10. The puppy lazily lies in the sun all afternoon.

Lesson 20 – Adverbs That Modify Verbs

An *adverb* changes a verb. A verb tells *what* the subject is doing. An *adverb* tells *how* the subject is doing that action. Most *adverbs* end with *-ly*.

 Complete each sentence using one of the *adverbs* listed.

boldly	perfectly	carefully	well
weakly	easily	rarely	quietly
softly	poorly	politely	loudly

1. Darnell _____ asked for a napkin.

2. Emmy _____ counted her allowance.

3. My mom and I cheered _____ during the concert.

4. The general _____ led his army into battle.

5. Speaking in public does not come _____ to me.

6. Kira's mom _____ buys junk food.

7. Enrique spelled all the words _____.

8. The robbers crept into the mansion _____.

9. Our family's dog _____ snored as she slept.

Lesson 20 – Adverbs That Modify Verbs

An *adverb* changes a verb. A verb tells *what* the subject is doing. An *adverb* tells *how* the subject is doing that action. Most *adverbs* end with *-ly*.

 Underline each *adverb* in the sentences.

1. Deanne quickly answered the question.

2. The baby slowly crawled up the steps.

3. Cars suddenly rolled into sight.

4. The vacuum steadily cleaned the carpets.

5. Students read their books closely.

6. I know a girl who plays the tuba well.

7. The pride of lions quietly followed their prey.

8. My family frantically cleaned the house.

 Underline each *adverb* in the paragraph.

The day of the big test had finally arrived. Students sat down at

their desks, nervously watching the teacher as she handed out booklets.

The students had waited for this day anxiously, and now, it was here.

Would they pass or fail? Hopefully, they would pass!

Lesson 20 – Adverbs That Modify Verbs

An **adverb** changes a verb. A verb tells *what* the subject is doing. An **adverb** tells *how* the subject is doing that action. Most **adverbs** end with *-ly*.

Complete each sentence with your own *adverb*.

1. The stray cats _____ hissed at the group of rats.

2. Kaden and his dog walked _____ around the block.

3. Teachers _____ prepared for their meeting.

4. Amira _____ counted her money.

5. A tornado _____ destroyed a farmhouse.

Complete the paragraph with your own *adverbs*.

   I went to the park. The sun shone _____.

Then, a boy jumped off the swing _____.

He _____ walked over to me. He asked if I

wanted to be his friend! I said yes! Now we _____

play at the park every day.

Lesson 20 – Adverbs That Modify Verbs

An *adverb* changes a verb. A verb tells *what* the subject is doing. An *adverb* tells *how* the subject is doing that action. Most *adverbs* end with *-ly*.

 Write sentences according to the instructions below. Use an *adverb* in each sentence and underline it.

1. Write a sentence about **a mouse eating cheese.**

_____

_____

2. Write a sentence about **rain falling on the ground.**

_____

_____

3. Write a sentence about **wind blowing through a canyon.**

_____

_____

4. Write a sentence about **a lion chasing its prey.**

_____

_____

STOP **Complete Assessment 8**

Lesson 21 – Pronoun/Antecedent Agreement

A **pronoun** is a word that can be used in place of a noun. The word that the pronoun replaces is called an **antecedent**. Pronouns need to agree with (or match) their antecedents in both gender and number.

X <u>Santa Claus</u> prepares <u>**her**</u> sleigh for Christmas.

> ***This pronoun does NOT agree with the antecedent.***

✓ <u>Santa Claus</u> prepares <u>**his**</u> sleigh for Christmas.

> ***Now the pronoun agrees with the antecedent.***

 Choose the *pronoun* that agrees with the underlined *antecedent*.

1. The <u>library</u> closes **(his / its)** doors at 8:00.

2. <u>Flowers</u> drop **(their / its)** petals.

3. <u>Amos</u> sweeps **(his / her)** kitchen.

4. The bright <u>sun</u> shines **(their / its)** rays.

5. <u>Georgia</u> gathers **(his / her)** books.

6. The <u>superheroes</u> grabbed **(their / his)** shields.

7. The <u>crew members</u> swung **(his / their)** wrecking ball.

8. <u>Kittens</u> snuggled in **(its / their)** basket.

9. After <u>Jared's</u> piano recital, **(she / he)** hugged **(her / his)** grandparents.

10. The <u>brothers</u> played **(his / their)** guitars like experts.

79

Lesson 21 – Pronoun/Antecedent Agreement

A *pronoun* is a word that can be used in place of a noun. The word that the pronoun replaces is called an *antecedent*. Pronouns need to agree with (or match) their antecedents in both gender and number.

List of Pronouns					
I	me	my	you	your	he
him	his	she	her	it	its
they	them	their	we	us	our

Complete the sentences with *pronouns*. Use *pronouns* that agree with (or match) the underlined *antecedents*.

1. Michael snuggled under the covers and listened to <u>his mother</u>.

_____ told Michael a story.

2. I met two <u>firemen</u> at the store today. _____

names were José and Nicholas.

3. Donald saw several <u>ducks</u> at the park. Donald broke off parts of his

sandwich and fed the bits to _____.

4. <u>My sister and I</u> saved twenty dollars. Then, <u>my sister and I</u> spent

_____ money on a new game.

5. I love my <u>Uncle Jerry</u>. _____ rides a motorcycle!

6. Mom and Dad gave Emma a new <u>book</u> for Christmas. Emma read

_____ right away!

80

Lesson 21 – Pronoun/Antecedent Agreement

A **pronoun** is a word that can be used in place of a noun. The word that the pronoun replaces is called an **antecedent**. Pronouns need to agree with (or match) their antecedents in both gender and number.

 Adam and Pete are friends. **His** _favorite game is basketball._

This pronoun does NOT agree with the antecedent.

 Adam and Pete are friends. **Their** _favorite game is basketball._

Now the pronoun agrees with the antecedent.

Choose the _pronoun_ that agrees with the underlined _antecedent_.

1. The <u>bee</u> flapped **(its / their)** wings.

2. The <u>men</u> lifted **(their / its)** hats.

3. <u>Gemma</u> gave **(his / her)** mom a hug.

4. <u>Curt and Max</u> washed **(their / his)** dog.

5. My <u>dad</u> dropped **(his / her)** shovel.

6. <u>Jim and Less</u> sent **(their / his)** sister a letter.

7. The <u>door</u> came off **(his / its)** hinges.

8. The <u>girls</u> saw **(her / their)** friends at the park.

9. Tess gave her <u>mom and dad</u> **(her / their)** money back.

10. <u>Dennis</u> raised **(his / him)** hand.

Try reading each sentence out loud. Which pronoun sounds the best?

Lesson 21 – Pronoun/Antecedent Agreement

A ***pronoun*** is a word that can be used in place of a noun. The word that the pronoun replaces is called an ***antecedent***. Pronouns need to agree with (or match) their antecedents in both gender and number.

List of Pronouns					
I	me	my	you	your	he
him	his	she	her	it	its
they	them	their	we	us	our

Complete the sentences with *pronouns*. Use *pronouns* that agree with (or match) the underlined *antecedents*.

1. The little <u>boy</u> called _____ mother.

2. I went to a music concert and went backstage to meet the <u>band members</u>. I got to shake _____ hands!

3. Cass tripped on the sidewalk and dropped his <u>books</u>! Now all _____ covers are scratched!

4. My <u>sister</u> was crying, so I gave _____ a tissue.

5. <u>Fred, George, and Ginny</u> are my cousins. _____ are a wild bunch!

6. <u>I</u> have two neighbors, Andy and Sid. Andy is _____ friend, but Sid doesn't like _____.

Lesson 21 – Pronoun/Antecedent Agreement

A *pronoun* is a word that can be used in place of a noun. The word that the pronoun replaces is called an *antecedent*. Pronouns need to agree with (or match) their antecedents in both gender and number.

*My **pets** are Joey and Sherlock. **They** are snobby cats.*

| antecedent | | pronoun |

Write sentences according to the instructions below. Circle the *antecedents* and underline the *pronouns* you use.

1. Write two sentences about **your pet**. Include an antecedent in the first sentence and a pronoun in the second.

_____

_____

_____

_____

2. Write two sentences about **your favorite food**. Include an antecedent in the first sentence and a pronoun in the second.

_____

_____

_____

_____

STOP Complete Assessment 9

Lesson 22 – Subject/Verb Agreement

In a sentence, the subject and the verb must agree with (or match) each other.

Singular subjects take *singular verbs*.

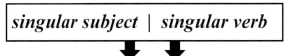

Jack jumps over the candlestick.

Plural subjects take *plural verbs*.

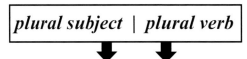

The children jump over the candlestick.

This is called *subject/verb agreement* because the subject and the verb match. Most of the time, *singular verbs* end with an -*s*, and *plural verbs* do not end with an -*s*.

 Circle the *verb* that agrees with the subject.

1. Marie **(attends / attend)** college in Warsaw.

2. She **(studies / study)** physics and chemistry.

3. Marie and her sister **(moves / move)** to Paris.

4. Then, Marie **(meets / meet)** Pierre Curie, who was also a scientist.

5. They **(marries / marry)** each other because they **(is / are)** in love.

 Circle the *subject* that agrees with the verb.

1. The **(sun / suns)** shines on the grassy field.

2. **(Flower / Flowers)** wave in the wind.

3. Spotted **(cow / cows)** quietly graze.

4. The **(farmer / farmers)** looks out over his land.

5. **(He / They)** loves the land because **(it / they)** is good.

Lesson 22 – Subject/Verb Agreement

When you use a **singular subject**, you must use a **singular verb**. In the same way, when you use a **plural subject**, you must use a **plural verb**. This is called **subject/verb agreement** because the subject and the verb match.

My puppy barks *a lot.*

singular subject and verb

My older dogs bark *less.*

plural subject and verb

 Fill in the blanks with verbs from the word bank. Remember to match *singular subjects* with *singular verbs* and *plural subjects* with *plural verbs*!

1. Dogs _____ at night.

2. The fox _____ a hole.

3. The boys _____ sorry.

4. Roses _____ in the spring.

5. Wind _____ the trees.

6. Jess and Sam _____ me gifts.

7. Music _____ the infant.

Singular	Plural
barks	bark
is	are
blows	blow
digs	dig
calms	calm
gives	give
blooms	bloom

Lesson 22 – Subject/Verb Agreement

When you use a *singular subject*, you must use a *singular verb*. In the same way, when you use a *plural subject*, you must use a *plural verb*. This is called *subject/verb agreement* because the subject and the verb match.

<u>**Jen sings**</u> *in the play.*

singular subject
and verb

<u>**The girls sing**</u> *together.*

plural subject
and verb

Most of the time, *singular verbs* end with an *-s*, and *plural verbs* do not end with an *-s*.

 Circle the *verb* that agrees with the subject.

1. The girls (**rolls** / **roll**) down the hill.

2. Susan (**stops** / **stop**) halfway down the slope.

3. The bushes (**is** / **are**) in her way and (**blocks** / **block**) her!

4. However, Callie (**reaches** / **reach**) the very bottom of the hill.

5. Susan (**runs** / **run**) the rest of the way, and Callie (**waits** / **wait**) for her.

 Circle the *subject* that agrees with the verb.

1. The (**panda** / **pandas**) rests against a stone.

2. (**Raindrop** / **Raindrops**) fall to the ground.

3. The (**bird** / **birds**) sing loudly in the trees.

4. The (**forest** / **forests**) is a peaceful place.

5. (**A photographer** / **Photographers**) captures the scene in a photo.

86

Lesson 22 – Subject/Verb Agreement

When you use a *singular subject*, you must use a *singular verb*. In the same way, when you use a *plural subject*, you must use a *plural verb*. This is called *subject/verb agreement* because the subject and the verb match.

The startled girl drops *the cake!*

The chefs and bakers drop *their pies!*

singular subject and verb

plural subject and verb

 Rewrite the sentences so that the *verbs* agree with their *subjects*.

1. The children runs at recess.

_____

2. Mel and Sara swims in the summer.

_____

3. Tanner build a house.

_____

4. The dishes falls from the shelf.

_____

5. Bells rings on Christmas day.

_____

6. My mom trim the rose bush.

_____

Lesson 23 – Contractions

Contractions are two words combined to make one shorter word. Contractions delete letters of one word and add an apostrophe.

These words are common in informal writing and speech. Most contractions are formed using *am, are, is, was, have, not, will,* and *would.*

let us – **let's**	can not – **can't**
I am – **I'm**	do not – **don't**
you are – **you're**	does not – **doesn't**
we are – **we're**	did not – **didn't**
they are – **they're**	is not – **isn't**
she is/was – **she's**	will not – **won't**
it is/was – **it's**	would not – **wouldn't**
who is/was – **who's**	are not – **aren't**
there is/was – **there's**	I will – **I'll**
what is/was – **what's**	you will – **you'll**
I have – **I've**	he will – **he'll**
you have – **you've**	it will – **it'll**
we have – **we've**	I would – **I'd**
could have – **could've**	you would – **you'd**
would have – **would've**	they would – **they'd**

Lesson 23 – Contractions

Contractions are two words combined to make one shorter word. Contractions delete letters of one word and add an apostrophe.

He is sleepy. ➡ *He's* sleepy.

Underline the *contractions* in the sentences below. Write the two words that are being combined on the blanks.

1. She'll sing all night.   _____ _____

2. Let's go home.   _____ _____

3. Cats don't like to get wet.   _____ _____

4. You're a good singer.   _____ _____

5. They'd leave if they could.   _____ _____

Rewrite the sentences and combine the two underlined words into a *contraction*.

1. Kim and Jon are not siblings.

_____

2. Who is at the door?

_____

3. I have never been so happy!

_____

Lesson 23 – Contractions

Contractions are two words combined to make one shorter word. Contractions delete letters of one word and add an apostrophe.

*The dog **will not** go outside.* *The dog **won't** go outside.*

 Write sentences according to the instructions below. Include a *contraction* in each sentence and underline it.

1. Write a sentence about **one of your friends.**

_____

_____

2. Write a sentence about **a rabbit.**

_____

_____

3. Write a sentence about **yourself.**

_____

_____

4. Write a sentence about **a song.**

_____

_____

Lesson 24 – Don't/Doesn't Problem

Don't is used with plural subjects and *doesn't* is used with singular subjects. Split the contractions into two words (do not, does not) to help know which contraction to use.

*Hector **don't** like peanut butter.* ➡ *Hector **do not** like peanut butter.* ✗

*Hector **doesn't** like peanut butter.* ➡ *Hector **does not** like peanut butter.* ✓

Write *don't* or *doesn't* to complete the sentence.

1. The new movie _____ come out until next week.

2. My friend _____ know if it will do well in theaters.

3. Critics say that they _____ like the movie.

4. They _____ think the story is good.

5. The story _____ make sense to the audience.

6. The producer _____ know if the movie will make money.

7. The actors _____ know if they'll be hired again.

8. The writers _____ know if the sequel will be made.

9. When the movie comes out, it _____ do well at all.

10. I guess people _____ want to see another movie about robots.

Lesson 24 – Don't/Doesn't Problem

Don't is used with plural subjects and *doesn't* is used with singular subjects. Split the contractions into two words (do not, does not) to help know which contraction to use.

For each sentence, split the contraction *don't* or *doesn't* into two words in the boxes. If the sentence has the correct contraction, write CORRECT on the line. If the sentence has the wrong contraction, rewrite the sentence on the lines provided so that the verbs agree with the nouns.

1. Mom and Dad <u>doesn't</u> like to go into town.

_____

_____

2. They <u>don't</u> like the traffic.

_____

_____

3. They <u>doesn't</u> like how noisy it is.

_____

_____

4. Mom really <u>don't</u> like shopping online.

_____

_____

5. They <u>doesn't</u> want to go to town.

_____

Lesson 24 – Don't/Doesn't Problem

Don't is used with plural subjects and *doesn't* is used with singular subjects. Split the contractions into two words (do not, does not) to help know which contraction to use.

<u>*A cat doesn't fly.*</u>   <u>*Cats don't fly.*</u>

| singular subject and verb | | plural subject and verb |

Write sentences according to the instructions below. Use *don't* or *doesn't* in each sentence.

1. Write a sentence about what **owls** do *not* do.

_____

_____

2. Write a sentence about what **a spinning top** does *not* do.

_____

_____

3. Write a sentence about what **a bear** does *not* do.

_____

_____

4. Write a sentence about what **a car** does *not* do.

_____

_____

STOP **Complete Assessment 11**

TOOLS FOR EFFECTIVE COMMUNICATION

✓ **Apply Parts of Speech**

✓ **Apply Sentence Structure**

Lesson 25 – Adjectives in Action

Adjectives are words that modify (change) and describe nouns. They are tools that writers use to communicate effectively with the reader.

Using **adjectives** in your writing helps your reader picture what you are writing about and makes your nouns more effective.

The girl faced the crowd.

The <u>scared</u> girl faced the <u>large</u> crowd.

Books lined the shelves of the library.

Books lined the <u>dusty</u> shelves of the <u>old</u> library.

Some adjectives are more descriptive than others. When you use **descriptive adjectives**, the reader sees exactly what you see because you are using imagery in your writing. Replacing vague adjectives with **descriptive adjectives** makes your writing more interesting.

The <u>red</u> cupcake smelled <u>good</u>.

The <u>crimson</u> cupcake smelled <u>delicious</u>.

She walked through the streets of the <u>cold</u> city with her <u>good</u> friend.

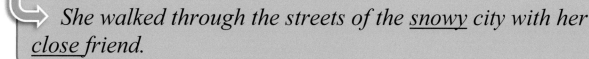
She walked through the streets of the <u>snowy</u> city with her <u>close</u> friend.

The <u>smart</u> lion followed its prey across the <u>yellow</u> grass.

The <u>clever</u> lion followed its prey across the <u>golden</u> grass.

Lesson 25 – Adjectives in Action

Adjectives are words that modify (or change) nouns. They are tools that writers use to communicate effectively with the reader.

Using *adjectives* in your writing helps your reader picture what you are writing about and makes your nouns more effective.

Choose adjectives wisely. Use a thesaurus to replace overused and vague adjectives!

Complete each sentence with a descriptive *adjective*.

1. _____ buffalo stampeded across the plain.

2. Donovan tried to tame his _____ hair.

3. _____ dancers leapt and twirled on the stage.

4. Make sure you pick the _____ flowers for Mom.

5. The joke I heard from Darius was _____!

6. Cherilyn's _____ dog is causing a lot of trouble.

7. _____ brownies waited for us on the counter.

8. Jerrica was _____, so she didn't want to visit the park.

9. I threw the _____ bag of trash into the dumpster.

Lesson 25 – Adjectives in Action

Adjectives are words that modify (or change) nouns. They are tools that writers use to communicate effectively with the reader. Some adjectives are more descriptive than others. Replacing vague adjectives with *descriptive adjectives* makes your writing more interesting.

 Circle the *adjective* that is more descriptive and interesting.

1. The kitchen table is **(old / ancient)**.

2. The **(joyful / happy)** students laughed.

3. Blake pets the **(nice / fuzzy)** kitten.

4. The television was **(blaring / loud)**.

5. The **(small / scrawny)** tree waved in the wind.

6. Kurt baked **(tasty / delicious)** cakes.

7. The **(pretty / colorful)** butterfly landed on a flower.

8. After my uncle cleaned his motorcycle, it looked **(clean / shiny)**.

9. The board game was **(difficult / hard)** to play.

10. Sandra straightens her **(frizzy / messy)** hair.

Lesson 25 – Adjectives in Action

Adjectives are words that modify (or change) nouns. They are tools that writers use to communicate effectively with the reader. Some adjectives are more descriptive than others. Replacing vague adjectives with ***descriptive adjectives*** makes your writing more interesting.

 The sentences below contain no *adjectives*. Make them more descriptive and interesting by rewriting them and adding *descriptive adjectives*. Some sentences may need more than one.

1. Kelly bought a house.

2. The house needed work.

3. The walls were a color.

4. Spiders hung from the lamps.

5. Kelly painted the walls a color.

6. She spent a week cleaning the house.

7. She loves her home.

Lesson 25 – Adjectives in Action

Adjectives are words that modify (or change) nouns. They are tools that writers use to communicate effectively with the reader. Some adjectives are more descriptive than others. Replacing vague adjectives with *descriptive adjectives* makes your writing more interesting.

 Read the paragraph below.

> Olivia owns a <u>small</u> pug. He has <u>nice</u> fur and a <u>funny</u> tail. Olivia takes the <u>small</u> pug on a walk. The pug has to move his <u>short</u> legs quickly to keep up! Liv gives the <u>happy</u> pug water after the <u>long</u> walk.

The paragraph will be more interesting with more descriptive adjectives! Rewrite the paragraph above and change the underlined adjectives to be more descriptive and interesting!

_____

_____

_____

_____

_____

_____

_____

Lesson 26 – Action Verbs in Action

Action verbs tell what the subject does. They are tools that writers use to communicate effectively with the reader.

Action verbs inform the reader what is happening in the sentence. Using *descriptive action verbs* makes your writing interesting to the reader.

Some *action verbs* do a better job than others at showing the reader the action of the sentence. The best *action verbs* show the reader the action, not just tell the reader the action.

Show!

Don't tell.

We went to my grandma's house and went in the pool.

> *We <u>drove</u> to my grandma's house and <u>swam</u> in the pool.*

Marko was excited when his parents said they were going to Disneyland!

> *Marko <u>squealed</u> and <u>danced</u> when his parents <u>announced</u> they were going to Disneyland!*

The wind was rough, and a lot of rain fell.

> *The wind <u>blustered</u> the trees, and rain <u>gushed</u> from the sky and <u>pounded</u> the ground.*

Edith saw her mother and ran to her. She gave her a big hug!

> *Edith <u>noticed</u> her mother and <u>dashed</u> to her. She <u>jumped</u> into her arms and <u>squeezed</u> her tight!*

Lesson 26 – Action Verbs in Action

Action verbs tell what the subject does. They are tools that writers use to communicate effectively with the reader. Using *descriptive action verbs* makes your writing interesting to the reader.

 Complete each sentence with a descriptive *action verb*.

1. The waiter _____ coffee with cream.

2. Hot water _____ on the stovetop.

3. Jesse _____ for his missing hat.

4. A cowboy _____ the wild stallion.

5. Tristan _____ the ball into the goal.

6. The giant oak _____ with a mighty thump.

7. Ani _____ a paper for class.

8. Kristen _____ the coin into the fountain.

9. Giant dragons _____ fire at the intruders.

10. Our neighbors _____ loud music all night long.

11. Playing an instrument _____ lots of practice.

Lesson 26 – Action Verbs in Action

Action verbs tell what the subject does. They are tools that writers use to communicate effectively with the reader. Using *descriptive action verbs* makes your writing interesting to the reader.

Some *action verbs* do a better job than others at showing the reader the action of the sentence. The best *action verbs* show the reader the action, not just tell the reader the action.

 Circle the *action verb* that is more descriptive and interesting.

1. The spy **(snuck / moved)** through the dark hallway.

2. Peyton **(put / shot)** the arrow into the bullseye.

> Descriptive action verbs show the reader what is happening in the sentence.

3. The white flag **(is / flapped)** in the wind.

4. Misha **(stared / looked)** at the lion.

5. The mother bear **(protected / stood by)** her cubs.

6. Otters **(are / paddle)** in the river.

7. The angry neighbor **(knocked / pounded)** on the door.

8. I accidentally **(took / ripped)** a page from the book!

9. Sam's dog **(barked / snarled)** at the intruder.

10 Abigail **(chose / got)** a chocolate cake for her party.

Lesson 26 – Action Verbs in Action

Action verbs tell what the subject does. They are tools that writers use to communicate effectively with the reader. Using *descriptive action verbs* makes your writing interesting to the reader.

 The sentences below contain no *action verbs*. Rewrite them by adding *descriptive action verbs* where indicated.

1. Char___her birthday.

_____

2. Her family___her out to dinner.

_____

3. The waitress___them at a big booth.

_____

4. They all___the menu.

_____

5. The restaurant___so much amazing food!

_____

6. Char finally___a burger and fries.

_____

7. Suddenly, all the wait staff___out.

_____

8. They___"Happy Birthday" to Char!

_____

Lesson 26 – Action Verbs in Action

Action verbs tell what the subject does. They are tools that writers use to communicate effectively with the reader. Using ***descriptive action verbs*** makes your writing interesting to the reader.

Some ***action verbs*** do a better job than others at showing the reader the action of the sentence. The best ***action verbs*** show the reader the action, not just tell the reader the action.

 Read the paragraph below.

An orange cat <u>was</u> in a tree. Then, a white cat <u>came</u> by. She <u>sat</u> on

the ground. The orange cat <u>went</u> out of the tree. He <u>went</u> to the white cat. She

<u>looked</u> at him. Then, they <u>sat</u> together as friends.

The paragraph will be more interesting with more descriptive action verbs! Rewrite the paragraph above and change the underlined action verbs to be more descriptive and interesting!

_____

_____

_____

_____

_____

_____

_____

Lesson 27 – Adverbs in Action

Adverbs change verbs. Most *adverbs* end with *-ly*. *Adverbs* describe verbs by telling the ready *how* the action is being done.

Adding *adverbs* to sentences makes your writing more descriptive and interesting. Look at how adding adverbs change the examples below:

Moira looked out the window.

> *Moira <u>anxiously</u> looked out the window.*

My brother handed over the present.

> *My brother <u>reluctantly</u> handed over the present.*

However, using too many *adverbs* can make your sentence confusing.

The car began to roll down the hill.

> *<u>Suddenly</u>, the car <u>quickly</u> began to roll down the hill <u>loudly</u>.*

Using the same *adverb* too many times can be confusing, too.

The vase fell. It cracked. Pieces flew across the floor. My mom screamed.

> *<u>Suddenly</u>, the vase fell. <u>Suddenly</u>, it cracked. Pieces <u>suddenly</u> flew across the floor. My mom <u>suddenly</u> screamed.*

Lesson 27 – Adverbs in Action

Adverbs change verbs. Most *adverbs* end with *-ly*. *Adverbs* describe verbs by telling the ready *how* the action is being done. Adding *adverbs* to sentences makes your writing more descriptive and interesting.

Complete each sentence with an *adverb*. Try not to use the same *adverb* more than once.

1. Our family _____ decorated the Christmas tree.

2. The crickets chirped _____ as the sun went down.

3. Lydia _____ packed her suitcase for the trip.

4. Trevor _____ finished his writing assignment.

5. The waiters cleaned up _____ after the dinner.

6. My sister _____ unwrapped her birthday presents.

7. The noisy geese _____ waddled across the road.

8. _____, rain poured down at the baseball game.

9. The carpenter _____ finished crafting the chairs.

10. "Why do you want to know?" asked Julie _____.

Lesson 27 – Adverbs in Action

Adverbs change verbs. Most *adverbs* end with -*ly*. *Adverbs* describe verbs by telling the ready *how* the action is being done. Adding *adverbs* to sentences makes your writing more descriptive and interesting.

However, using too many *adverbs* can make your sentence confusing. Using the same *adverb* too many times can be confusing, too.

 The sentences below contain no *adverbs*. Rewrite them and make them more descriptive by adding *adverbs*.

1. An elf named Jerry worked for Santa Claus.

_____

2. He created toys like the other elves.

_____

3. Jerry dreamed of a different job.

_____

4. He wanted to become a dentist.

_____

5. The other elves made fun of Jerry.

_____

6. They told him that his dream was silly.

_____

7. Even Santa rejected Jerry's dream.

_____

8. Jerry refused to give up.

_____

Lesson 28 – Writing Items in a Series

A *series* is a small list of three or more words within a sentence. *Commas* separate items in a *series*. A *series* may be a list of nouns or verbs.

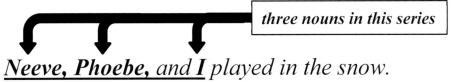

three nouns in this series

Neeve, Phoebe, and I played in the snow.

Add the missing *commas* to the *series* in the sentences below.

1. Nouns can be a person place or thing.

2. June July and August are all summer months.

3. Stories have characters places and events.

4. Asia Europe and Africa are all continents.

5. Decorate the tree with ornaments ribbons and glitter.

6. Use pecans walnuts or peanuts in the brownies.

7. We ate cake ice cream and cookies at the party.

8. Jake Trey and Michael are coming over later.

9. We are bringing salad burgers and pie to the picnic.

Lesson 28 – Writing Items in a Series

A *series* is a small list of three or more words within a sentence. *Commas* separate items in a *series*. A *series* may be a list of nouns or verbs.

three nouns in this series

Tigers, penguins, and ostriches *live at the zoo.*

Fill in the blanks below with nouns. Add the missing commas.

1. I received _____ _____ and

_____ for my birthday.

2. Kaden won't eat _____

_____ or _____.

3. My sister played _____ _____

and _____ for the concert.

4. _____ _____ and

_____ are my favorite colors.

5. _____ _____ and

_____ are the fastest animals!

Lesson 28 – Writing Items in a Series

A *series* is a small list of three or more words within a sentence. *Commas* separate items in a *series*. A *series* may be a list of nouns or verbs.

three verbs in this series

The horse **neighed, whinnied, and snorted**.

✎ **Add the missing *commas* to the *series* in the sentences below.**

1. The girl coughed sneezed and sniffed.

2. Sweep mop and scrub the bathroom floor.

3. We prepared mixed and baked the gingerbread.

4. The student writes checks and prints his paper.

5. Our dog barks growls and howls at passing cats.

6. Do all your family members sketch draw and paint?

7. Sort fold and put away the laundry.

8. The dancer leaps twirls and glides across the stage.

9. Carlos bites chews and swallows the ginger cookie.

Lesson 28 – Writing Items in a Series

A *series* is a small list of three or more words within a sentence. *Commas* separate items in a *series*. A *series* may be a list of nouns or verbs.

three verbs in this series

*The phone **buzzes, beeps, and rings**.*

Fill in the blanks below with verbs. Add the missing commas.

1. The soldiers _____

_____ and _____ .

2. I never _____

_____ or _____ .

3. The animals _____

_____ and _____ in the barnyard.

4. _____ _____ and

_____ the muddy car.

5. On Saturdays, I _____ _____

and _____ .

Lesson 28 – Writing Items in a Series

A *series* is a small list of three or more words within a sentence. *Commas* separate items in a *series*. A *series* may be a list of nouns or verbs.

Write sentences according to the instructions below. Include a *series* of verbs or nouns in each sentence.

1. Write a sentence about **your favorite foods.**

_____

_____

2. Write a sentence about **three things you are good at.**

_____

_____

3. Write a sentence about **your favorite holidays.**

_____

_____

4. Write a sentence about **what you do after school.**

_____

_____

STOP **Complete Assessment 12**

Lesson 29 – Simple and Compound Sentences

A *simple sentence* is a single sentence that includes one subject and one predicate. A *compound sentence* is made up of two or more simple sentences combined to make one big sentence. A *comma* and *conjunction* are used to combine the two simple sentences. A *conjunction* is a joining word.

Cats catch mice.

simple sentence

Cats catch mice, and owls hunt rats.

compound sentence

Identify the following sentences as *simple* or *compound*. If the sentence is simple, write an "S"; if it is compound, write a "C."

1. Frogs are neat animals. _____

2. Frogs can swim, and they can live on land! _____

3. Baby frogs are called tadpoles. _____

4. Tadpoles look like fish, but they are just frogs. _____

5. Tadpoles can grow into frogs in one day. _____

6. That is amazing! _____

7. Most frogs eat bugs, yet some frogs eat fruit. _____

8. Frogs live by ponds, or they live in trees. _____

9. Some people eat frogs. _____

10. Would you try a frog, or would you skip that meal? _____

Lesson 29 – Simple and Compound Sentences

A *simple sentence* is a single sentence that includes one subject and one predicate. A *compound sentence* is made up of two or more simple sentences combined to make one big sentence. A *comma* and *conjunction* are used to combine the two simple sentences. A *conjunction* is a joining word.

The concert is expensive.   *The concert is expensive, **yet** I want to attend.*

simple sentence   compound sentence

Combine the sentences below using a *comma* and a *conjunction*.

Conjunctions
and, but, or, nor, so, for, yet

1. The donkey is hungry. He eats some grass.

_____

2. The grass is delicious. The donkey is still hungry.

_____

3. He searches for other food. He cannot find any.

_____

4. Geri fixes toys. He has done this for a long time.

_____

5. Some toys are delicate. Geri is careful.

_____

6. Geri owns his own shop. He is popular.

_____

Lesson 29 – Simple and Compound Sentences

A *simple sentence* is a single sentence that includes one subject and one predicate. A *compound sentence* is made up of two or more simple sentences combined to make one big sentence. A *comma* and *conjunction* are used to combine the two simple sentences. A *conjunction* is a joining word.

Conjunctions
and, but, or, nor, so, for, yet

 Write sentences according the instructions below.

1. Write a *simple sentence* about a dog.

_____

_____

2. Write a *simple sentence* about the person who owns the dog.

_____

_____

3. Combine the two sentences you wrote above into a *compound sentence.* Don't forget to use a *comma* and a *conjunction.*

_____

_____

_____

_____

115

Lesson 29 – Simple and Compound Sentences

A *simple sentence* is a single sentence that includes one subject and one predicate. A *compound sentence* is made up of two or more simple sentences combined to make one big sentence. A *comma* and *conjunction* are used to combine the two simple sentences. A *conjunction* is a joining word.

I had pasta for lunch.   *I had pasta for lunch,* **but** *I want steak for dinner.*

| simple sentence | compound sentence |

Identify the following sentences as simple or compound. If the sentence is simple, write an "S"; if it is compound, write a "C."

1. I like reading about cats. _____

2. Cats hunt alone, but they spend time with other cats. _____

3. Cats hunt birds, mice, and rats. _____

4. My mom is allergic to cats, so we have a dog instead. _____

Combine the sentences below using a *comma* and a *conjunction*.

| **Conjunctions** |
| and, but, or, nor, so, for, yet |

1. The rat is hungry. It wants some food.

_____

2. My brother is tall. I am short.

_____

3. Grandpa likes fishing. He likes hiking, too.

_____

4. Jan buys crackers. She buys yogurt.

_____

Lesson 29 – Simple and Compound Sentences

A *simple sentence* is a single sentence that includes one subject and one predicate. A *compound sentence* is made up of two or more simple sentences combined to make one big sentence. A *comma* and *conjunction* are used to combine the two simple sentences. A *conjunction* is a joining word.

Conjunctions
and, but, or, nor, so, for, yet

 Write sentences according the instructions below.

1. Write a *simple sentence* about a fish.

_____

_____

2. Write a *simple sentence* about the person who caught the fish.

_____

_____

3. Combine the two sentences you wrote above into a *compound sentence*. Don't forget to use a *comma* and a *conjunction*.

_____

_____

_____

_____

STOP Complete Assessment 13

Lesson 30 – Incomplete Sentences

An *incomplete sentence* is missing a subject or a predicate. Sometimes, a sentence is incomplete because it is not a complete thought. *Incomplete sentences* are also called *fragments*.

Missing a Subject	If a sentence only has a predicate, a subject must be added to make it complete.
	Flew away. ⟹ **The owl** *flew away.*

Missing a Predicate	If a sentence only has a subject, a predicate must be added to make it complete
	My dad. ⟹ *My dad* **washed the car.**

After writing a sentence, ask yourself these three questions:

Does the sentence have a subject?

Does the sentence have a predicate?

Does the sentence make sense?

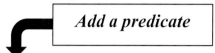

Lesson 30 – Incomplete Sentences

An *incomplete sentence* is missing a subject or a predicate. Sometimes, a sentence is incomplete because it is not a complete thought. *Incomplete sentences* are also called *fragments*.

> **Add a predicate**

The friends. ➡ *The friends* **attend a party**.

 The sentences below are *incomplete*. Write "S" if the sentences are missing a *subject* and "P" if they are missing a *predicate*.

1. My grandmother.   **What is missing?** _____

2. Closed the door.   **What is missing?** _____

3. The fluffy poodle.   **What is missing?** _____

4. Pauline.   **What is missing?** _____

5. Painted the bathroom.   **What is missing?** _____

6. Boiled some water.   **What is missing?** _____

 Underline the *incomplete sentence* in the paragraph below.

Alexis likes to sing. She is talented. Performs with a band. They play every Saturday. People enjoy listening to her!

 Correct the *incomplete sentence* on the line below.

_____

Lesson 30 – Incomplete Sentences

An *incomplete sentence* is missing a subject or a predicate. Sometimes, a sentence is incomplete because it is not a complete thought. *Incomplete sentences* are also called *fragments*.

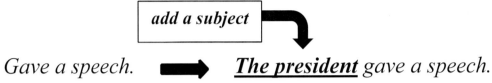

add a subject

Gave a speech. ➡ *The president* gave a speech.

Correct the *incomplete sentences* on the lines provided.

1. Fixed the computer.

_____

2. Ate fish tacos.

_____

3. The angry elephant.

_____

4. Big, fluffy pillows.

_____

5. The group of mothers.

_____

6. Searched for the remote.

_____

Lesson 30 – Incomplete Sentences

An ***incomplete sentence*** is missing a subject or a predicate. Sometimes, a sentence is incomplete because it is not a complete thought. ***Incomplete sentences*** are also called ***fragments***.

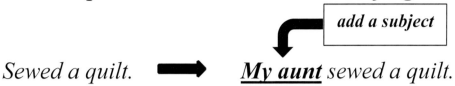

Sewed a quilt. ➡ <u>***My aunt***</u> *sewed a quilt.*

 The sentences below are *incomplete*. Write "S" if the sentences are missing a *subject* and "P" if they are missing a *predicate*.

1. Thanked the waiter.   **What is missing?** _____

2. The ratty towel.   **What is missing?** _____

3. Gathered all the leaves.   **What is missing?** _____

4. Plugged in a lamp.   **What is missing?** _____

5. A blank notebook.   **What is missing?** _____

6. The singing mermaid.   **What is missing?** _____

7. Sped away.   **What is missing?** _____

 Underline the *incomplete sentence* in the paragraph below.

Idris has a cold. He eats soup. Blows his nose. He stays home from school. Colds are no fun.

 Correct the *incomplete sentence* on the line below.

_____

Lesson 30 – Incomplete Sentences

An ***incomplete sentence*** is missing a subject or a predicate. Sometimes, a sentence is incomplete because it is not a complete thought. ***Incomplete sentences*** are also called ***fragments***.

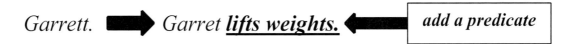

Garrett. ➡ *Garret **lifts weights.*** ⬅ add a predicate

 Correct the *incomplete sentences* on the lines provided.

1. The brick house.

_____

2. Ate too much cake.

_____

3. A huge dog.

_____

Sometimes a sentence with a subject and a predicate can still be ***incomplete*** because it is an ***incomplete thought***.

Because *Jenna doesn't like ice cream.*

 Words like this can make sentences incomplete thoughts.

Using beginning words like *because, before, after, when,* and *if* can make a sentence an ***incomplete thought***.

 Underline the *incomplete sentences* below.

1. We planted tulips.

2. Because Aimee is angry.

3. If you don't want to.

Lesson 31 – Run-On Sentences

A ***run-on sentence*** is two or more complete sentences (thoughts) written as a single sentence.

Run-on sentences can be corrected by separating the thought into two complete sentences with a punctuation mark, or by combining the sentences into a compound sentence.

Two Sentences	A run-on sentence can be corrected by separating the thoughts into two complete sentences with a punctuation mark.
	Mom likes chocolate I like vanilla. → *Mom likes chocolate. I like vanilla.*

Compound Sentence	A run-on sentence can be corrected by combining the sentences into a compound sentence.
	Mom likes chocolate I like vanilla. → *Mom likes chocolate, **but** I like vanilla.*

Lesson 31 – Run-On Sentences

A *run-on sentence* is two or more complete sentences (thoughts) written as a single sentence. **Run-on sentences** can be corrected by separating the sentences into two sentences with a punctuation mark, or by combining the sentences into a compound sentence.

The dog barks he wants outside. ➡ *The dog barks. He wants outside.*

 Underline each *run-on sentence*.

1. Scarlet went to a new school she didn't know anyone.

2. The teachers were kind she wanted friends.

3. One day, Scarlet saw a sign for choir try-outs.

4. She enjoyed singing she should sign up.

5. She might make friends in the choir.

 Underline the *run-on sentences* in the paragraph.

I learned to sew last week. My mom showed me how to use a needle and thread. I poked myself with the needle it hurt! I have made a dress and a vest they are both red. I will make a tablecloth next it will be blue. Sewing is so much fun!

Lesson 31 – Run-On Sentences

A *run-on sentence* is two or more complete sentences (thoughts) written as a single sentence. *Run-on sentences* can be corrected by separating the sentences into two sentences with a punctuation mark, or by combining the sentences into a compound sentence.

The bird sings it is spring. ➡ *The bird sings. It is spring.*

Correct each *run-on sentence* by making it into *two separate sentences*. Don't forget to use correct punctuation and capitalization.

1. I have friends we play together.

_____

_____

2. My brother likes to run he is fast.

_____

_____

3. Kendra found a penny she put it in her pocket.

_____

_____

4. My mom makes French toast it is good.

_____

_____

Lesson 31 – Run-On Sentences

A *run-on sentence* is two or more complete sentences (thoughts) written as a single sentence. *Run-on sentences* can be corrected by separating the sentences into two sentences with a punctuation mark, or by combining the sentences into a compound sentence.

The man dropped his hat it is lost. ➡️ *The man dropped his hat, so it is lost.*

 Underline each *run-on sentence*.

1. Ken plays the drums he is so loud.

2. Bess and Lin are dancers, and they practice often.

3. Snow falls on the ground it is pretty.

4. The camel drinks it will not be thirsty.

5. Jon is from France, so he speaks French.

 Underline the *run-on sentences* in the paragraph.

Chance and Philip were brothers. They played football at different schools. Their teams were pitted against each other. Chance and Philip didn't want to play they had no choice. Their coaches made them play. Philip found Chance before the game. He promised to be careful Chance promised the same thing. The game was exciting. No one was hurt. Chance and Philip were happy. Teams are important. Family, however, is more important.

Lesson 31 – Run-On Sentences

A *run-on sentence* is two or more complete sentences (thoughts) written as a single sentence. *Run-on sentences* can be corrected by separating the sentences into two sentences with a punctuation mark, or by combining the sentences into a compound sentence.

The sun shines the flowers bloom. ➡ *The sun shines, **and** the flowers bloom.*

Correct each *run-on sentence* by making it into a *compound sentence*. Don't forget to add a *comma* and a *conjunction*.

1. Liz walked in the rain her dress got muddy.

_____

_____

2. Her mother was upset she did not want to wash it.

_____

_____

3. Her mother used a special soap the stains came out.

_____

_____

4. Liz wears play clothes in the rain her dress stays clean.

_____

_____

Lesson 31 – Run-On Sentences

A *run-on sentence* is two or more complete sentences (thoughts) written as a single sentence. *Run-on sentences* can be corrected by separating the sentences into two sentences with a punctuation mark, or by combining the sentences into a compound sentence.

 Underline the *run-on sentences* in the paragraph below.

Seth's little sister is turning seven. Seth tries to find her a gift he goes to the store. He looks at games and toys he does not find a gift. He goes to a pet store across the street he looks at animals. He buys a white kitten and brings it home. His sister loves her new pet!

Rewrite this paragraph and correct each *run-on sentence*.

_____

_____

_____

_____

_____

_____

STOP Complete Assessment 14

Complete Unit One
Comprehensive Assessment

UNIT TWO: COMPOSITION

Lesson 32 – The Writing Process

To write well, follow *the writing process*. The writing process has five steps: *brainstorm*, *organize*, *draft*, *revise*, and *final draft*.

BRAINSTORM

First, choose a topic.

Write down many ideas. Narrow the ideas down, then choose one idea to be your topic.

ORGANIZE

Second, make a plan.

Plan what you will write before you begin to write. Use a graphic organizer to help organize your ideas.

DRAFT

Third, put your ideas in order.

Use your plan to begin writing. Put all your ideas into words on paper. The draft does not have to be perfect.

REVISE

Fourth, revise your draft.

Look for parts of your draft that you can improve. Add or change details, words, or sentences to improve your writing.

FINAL DRAFT

Fifth, edit your work and create a final copy.

Make sure capitalization and punctuation are correct and all words are spelled correctly. Re-record your writing and publish your final draft.

Lesson 33 – The Writing Process
Brainstorm

The first step in the writing process is ***brainstorm***.

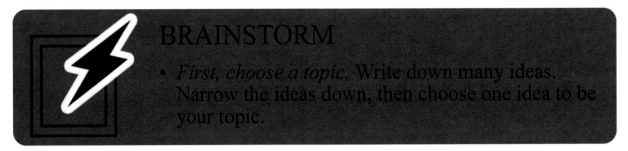

BRAINSTORM
- *First, choose a topic.* Write down many ideas. Narrow the ideas down, then choose one idea to be your topic.

Prompt

- *Imagine you are in charge of a zoo. In a paragraph, write about what animal you would spend the most time with and what you would do with it.*

First, list many different zoo animals in the box below.

Next, choose three animals from the list and record them in the boxes below.

Finally, draw a line through two animals and record your final choice in the box below.

Your Topic

Lesson 34 – The Writing Process
Organize

The second step in the writing process is *organize*.

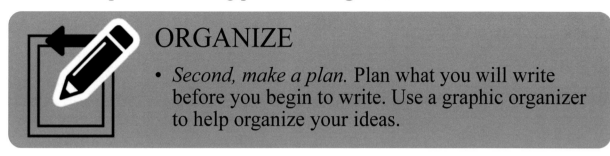

ORGANIZE

- *Second, make a plan.* Plan what you will write before you begin to write. Use a graphic organizer to help organize your ideas.

Plan what you will write for the opening, body, and closing of your paragraph.

- The opening should tell the reader what your topic is.

- The body should tell the reader details about your topic.

- The closing should close the paragraph.

A plan will help you when you start to write.

Do not use complete sentences in your plan. Instead, write simple terms and ideas.

Prompt

- *Imagine you are in charge of a zoo. In a paragraph, write about what animal you would spend the most time with and what you would do with it.*

Record your topic from the previous lesson.

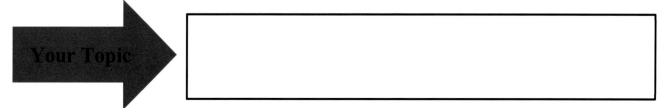

Lesson 34 – The Writing Process
Organize

The second step in the writing process is *organize*.

Use the graphic organizer to plan your paragraph about your topic.

Write ideas for the beginning of your paragraph. Write what your topic is.

Opening

Write ideas for the middle of your paragraph. Write details about your topic.

Detail

Detail

Detail

Write ideas for the end of your paragraph. Close your topic.

Closing

Lesson 35 – The Writing Process
Draft

The third step in the writing process is *draft*.

DRAFT

- *Third, put your ideas in order.* Use your plan to begin writing. Put all your ideas into words on paper. The draft does not have to be perfect.

O	*spend time with monkey*
D	*fun-loving and exciting*
D	*play games and teach tricks*
D	*swing on the play sets with them*
C	*monkey is awesome*

The *opening sentence* should:
- begin your composition
- introduce your topic

Look at how the graphic organizer above is turned into a paragraph:

If I owned a zoo, I would spend time with the monkeys. They are fun-loving and exciting. I would play games and teach tricks. I would swing on the play sets with them. Monkeys are awesome.

Lesson 35 – The Writing Process
Draft

The third step in the writing process is **draft**.

In a draft, take the ideas from your plan and make them complete sentences.

At this step of the writing process, your writing does not have to be perfect. Instead, try to make your ideas clear.

Prompt

- *Imagine you are in charge of a zoo. In a paragraph, write about what animal you would spend the most time with and what you would do with it.*

Draft your paragraph. Use the ideas from your plan

_____

_____

_____

_____

_____

_____

_____

_____

_____

Lesson 36 – The Writing Process Revise

The fourth step in the writing process is *revise*.

REVISE

- *Fourth, revise your draft.* Look for parts of your draft that you can improve. Add or change details, words, or sentences to improve your writing.

Look for ways to add descriptive adjectives and action verbs to your writing. If your sentences all begin with the same word, look for ways to use different beginning words.

Remember, you do not have to change *everything* you have written. Only make changes that *improve* your writing.

Draft
I would play games and teach tricks.

Revised
I would play games with them like Tag, and I would teach them tricks.

Revise your draft. Read your draft out loud, and touch each word as you read. Look for ways to add or change details, words, or sentences.

- Reading out loud will help you notice details you do not see when you read silently.
- Touching each word will help you focus on one thing at a time.

Read your draft out loud, and touch each word as you read.

☐   **Revised words**

☐   **Revised sentences**

Lesson 37 – The Writing Process
Final Draft

The last step in the writing process is *final draft*.

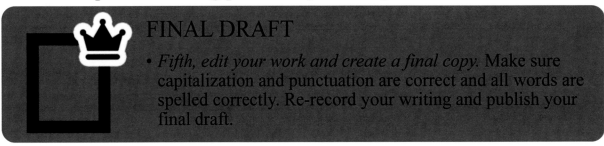

FINAL DRAFT

- *Fifth, edit your work and create a final copy.* Make sure capitalization and punctuation are correct and all words are spelled correctly. Re-record your writing and publish your final draft.

Make a **copy** of your revised draft on a new piece of paper. **Edit** your writing to make sure capitalization, punctuation, and spelling are correct.

Copy your revised draft on the lines below.

_____

_____

_____

_____

_____

_____

_____

_____

Read your final draft out loud, and touch each word as you read. Correct all capitalization, punctuation, and spelling errors.

☐ **Corrected capitalization errors**

☐ **Corrected punctuation errors**

☐ **Corrected spelling errors**

STOP **Complete Assessment 15**

Lesson 38 – Parts of a Paragraph

A *paragraph* is a group of sentences. It has three parts:

- **opening sentence**
- **body sentences**
- **closing sentence**

The first line of a paragraph has an *indent*. An indent is a space before the first sentence.

Indent →

Opening Sentence

I like to go outside on rainy days.

Body Sentences

I wear my raincoat and boots. My brother comes with me. We splash in the big puddles! It is fun.

Closing Sentence

Rainy days are great.

The *opening sentence* is the first sentence in a paragraph. It tells the reader what your paragraph will be about.

The *body sentences* are in the middle of a paragraph. This is where you give details about your topic.

The *closing sentence* is the last sentence in a paragraph. This is where you end your paragraph.

Lesson 38 – Parts of a Paragraph
Indent and Opening Sentence

An *indent* is the space before the first sentence of a paragraph. To make an *indent*, put your finger on the left margin of your paper and start your first sentence to the right of your finger.

The *opening sentence* is the first sentence in your paragraph. It contains the main idea of the paragraph.

 Circle the best *opening sentence* for a paragraph about thunderstorms.

A. I live in Kansas.

B. Thunderstorms are loud and scary.

C. My brother doesn't like it when it rains.

D. Fried chicken is tasty.

 The paragraph below is missing an *opening sentence*. Write an *opening sentence* in the blank that tells what the paragraph is about. Don't forget an indent!

_____

_____

_____ Cheetahs can

run as fast as a car. Their fur is golden with brown spots. These

big cats live in Africa. Cheetahs are very interesting animals!

Lesson 38 – Parts of a Paragraph
Body Sentences

Body sentences are in the middle of a paragraph. The body sentences contain details about the topic. They come after the *opening sentence*.

 Circle the body sentence that does *not* belong with the following opening sentence.

Opening sentence: Trips to the beach are fun!

A. I like to swim in the ocean.

B. My family builds sandcastles.

C. I collect seashells.

D. My dog is named Peach.

 The paragraph below is missing *body sentences*. Write *body sentences* that contain details about the topic in the opening sentence. Write at least three *body sentences*.

I want a dog. _____

_____

_____

_____

_____

_____ A dog is a great pet!

Lesson 38 – Parts of a Paragraph
Closing Sentence

The *closing sentence* is the last sentence in a paragraph. Like the opening sentence, the *closing sentence* contains the main topic of the paragraph. It brings the paragraph to a close. The *closing sentence* is very similar to the opening sentence.

 Circle the best *closing sentence* for a paragraph with the following opening sentence.

Opening sentence: My family took a fun trip to the fair.

A. Cotton candy is amazing!

B. Our trip to the fair was fun.

C. The fair had a roller coaster.

D. I like to read.

 The paragraph below is missing a *closing sentence*. Write a *closing sentence* in the blank to end the paragraph.

I like to learn about the moon. The moon orbits our planet. It is a big rock with craters and mountains. The moon shines at night. It reflects the light from the sun. People have walked on the moon, but no one lives there._____

_____

Lesson 39 – Staying on Topic

For your reader to understand your paragraph, you must stay on topic. ***Staying on topic*** means that your paragraph will only have sentences that include details about the topic.

> *My grandpa likes to go fishing. He fishes on a boat with a fishing pole. I like to fish with him.* ***My grandma likes to paint.*** *My grandpa is good at fishing.*
>
> **Off topic!**

 Choose the sentence that does *not* belong in a paragraph about instruments.

A. Trumpets are brass instruments.

B. People play different kinds of instruments.

C. I like pianos best.

D. Singers are very talented.

Hmm... Something does not belong.

 Underline the sentence that does *not* belong in the paragraph below.

My sister and I built a tire swing. We found a tire in my dad's workshop. Dad helped us tie it to a tree branch. I am eight years old. We swung for a long time. We had fun on the tire swing!

Lesson 39 – Staying on Topic

 Lucas is writing about his friend Mark. Read the opening and closing sentences of Lucas's paragraph. Help Lucas finish his paragraph by writing *three body sentences* that belong in the paragraph. Remember to stay on topic!

Mark likes to draw._____

_____

_____

_____

_____

_____Mark enjoys drawing pictures.

 Write *three* sentences that do not belong in the paragraph. These sentences do not stay on topic.

_____

_____

_____

_____

Lesson 39 – Staying on Topic

 Stacy is writing about board games. Read the opening and closing sentences of Stacy's paragraph. Help Stacey finish her paragraph by writing *three body sentences* that belong in the paragraph. Remember to stay on topic!

Board games are fun to play! _____

_____

_____

_____

_____

_____ Games are so much fun!

Write *three* sentences that do not belong in the paragraph. These sentences do not stay on topic.

_____

_____

_____

_____

Lesson 40 – Paragraph Practice
Brainstorm

Remember the *writing process* when you write paragraphs. The first step of the writing process is *brainstorm*.

 Brainstorm to choose a topic. Write down many ideas. Narrow the ideas down, then choose one idea to be your topic.

Prompt

- *If you had fifty dollars, how would you spend it? Would you buy something? Would you take a trip? Would you give it away? Write a paragraph explaining what you would do with fifty dollars.*

First, list many different ways you could spend fifty dollars in the box below.

Next, choose three options from the list and record them in the boxes below.

Finally, draw a line through two options and record your final choice in the box below.

Lesson 40 – Paragraph Practice
Organize

The second step in the writing process is *organize*. Make a plan for an *opening sentence, body sentences,* and a *closing sentence.*

Use the graphic organizer to plan your paragraph about your topic.

Write ideas for the beginning of your paragraph. Write what your topic is.

Opening

Write ideas for the middle of your paragraph. Write details about your topic.

Detail

Detail

Detail

Write ideas for the end of your paragraph. Close your topic.

Closing

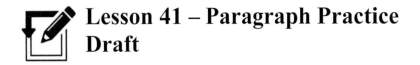

Lesson 41 – Paragraph Practice
Draft

The third step in the writing process is *draft*. In a draft, take the ideas from your plan and make them complete sentences.

At this step of the writing process, your writing does not have to be perfect. Instead, try to make your ideas clear.

Draft your paragraph. Use the ideas from your plan.

_____

_____

_____

_____

_____

_____

_____

_____

_____

_____

_____

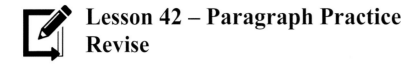 **Lesson 42 – Paragraph Practice**
Revise

The fourth step in the writing process is *revise*.

Look for ways to add descriptive adjectives and action verbs to your writing. If your sentences all begin with the same word, look for ways to use different beginning words.

Remember, you do not have to change *everything* you have written. Only make changes that *improve* your writing.

Draft
My shoes now are old.

Revised
My shoes I am wearing now are very old and torn.

Revise your draft. Read your draft out loud, and touch each word as you read. Look for ways to add or change details, words, or sentences.

- Reading out loud will help you notice details you do not see when you read silently.
- Touching each word will help you focus on one thing at a time.

Read your draft out loud, and touch each word as you read.

☐ **Revised words**

☐ **Revised sentences**

Lesson 43 – Paragraph Practice
Final Draft

The last step in the writing process is *final draft*.

Make a **copy** of your revised draft on a new piece of paper. **Edit** your writing to make sure capitalization, punctuation, and spelling are correct.

Copy your revised draft on the lines below.

_____

_____

_____

_____

_____

_____

_____

_____

_____

Read your final draft out loud, and touch each word as you read. Correct all capitalization, punctuation, and spelling errors.

☐ **Corrected capitalization errors**

☐ **Corrected punctuation errors**

☐ **Corrected spelling errors**

Paragraph Practice
Checklist

Indent and Opening Sentence

☐ Did you indent your opening sentence?

☐ Did you write an opening sentence?

☐ Does your opening sentence introduce the topic?

Body Sentences

☐ Did you write three or more body sentences?

☐ Does each sentence begin with a different word?

☐ Did you stay on topic?

Closing Sentence

☐ Did you write a closing sentence?

☐ Does the closing sentence end your topic?

Overall

☐ Did you use descriptive adjectives?

☐ Did you use descriptive action verbs?

☐ Did you use descriptive adverbs (when appropriate)?

Mechanics

☐ Did you check your spelling?

☐ Did you use capitalization correctly?

☐ Did you use punctuation correctly?

STOP **Complete Assessment 16**

Lesson 44 – Expository Paragraph

Expository writing explains, describes, or informs.

Expository writing **explains.**	→	*Explaining* is telling your reader how something works or how to do something.
Expository writing **describes.**	→	*Describing* is giving details to your reader that paint a picture of your topic.
Expository writing **informs.**	→	*Informing* is giving new information to your reader.

Look at this example of an *expository paragraph*. This paragraph is answering the prompt: *What is your favorite movie? Explain why you like this movie.*

> The opening sentence *informs* the reader about the writer's favorite movie.

My favorite movie is *Incredibles 2*. This movie is about a superhero family. I like Dash. He can run very fast, and he is also funny. The movie is exciting because the superheroes fight a villain! I like exciting movies. I really like the movie *Incredibles 2*.

> The details *explain* why the writer likes the movie.

Lesson 44 – Expository Paragraph
Brainstorm

Expository writing explains, describes, or informs.

 Brainstorm to choose a topic. Write down many ideas. Narrow the ideas down, then choose one idea to be your topic.

Prompt

• *Think about something you own that is important to you. What is this thing, and why is it valuable? In a paragraph, explain why this item is important to you.*

First, list many valuable things that you own.

Next, choose three items from the list and record them in the boxes below.

Finally, draw a line through two items and record your final choice in the box below.

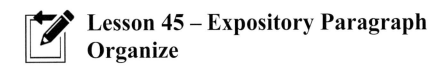 **Lesson 45 – Expository Paragraph**
Organize

Make a plan for an *opening sentence, body sentences,* and a *closing sentence.*

Use the graphic organizer to plan your paragraph about your topic.

Write ideas for the beginning of your paragraph. Write what your topic is.

Opening

Write ideas for the middle of your paragraph. Write details about your topic.

Detail

Detail

Detail

Write ideas for the end of your paragraph. Close your topic.

Closing

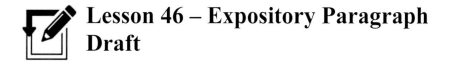 **Lesson 46 – Expository Paragraph
Draft**

In a draft, take the ideas from your plan and make them complete sentences.

At this step of the writing process, your writing does not have to be perfect. Instead, try to make your ideas clear.

Draft your paragraph. Use the ideas from your plan.

_____

_____

_____

_____

_____

_____

_____

_____

_____

_____

_____

_____

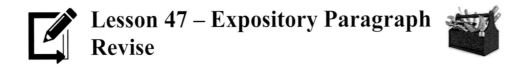

Lesson 47 – Expository Paragraph Revise

Look for ways to add descriptive adjectives and action verbs to your writing. If your sentences all begin with the same word, look for ways to use different beginning words.

Remember, you do not have to change *everything* you have written. Only make changes that ***improve*** your writing.

Draft
It has my voice sing.

Revised
On the tape, I can be heard singing as a child.

Revise your draft. Read your draft out loud, and touch each word as you read. Look for ways to add or change details, words, or sentences.

- Reading out loud will help you notice details you do not see when you read silently.
- Touching each word will help you focus on one thing at a time.

Read your draft out loud, and touch each word as you read.

☐ **Revised words**

☐ **Revised sentences**

Lesson 48 – Expository Paragraph
Final Draft

Make a **copy** of your revised draft on a new piece of paper. **Edit** your writing to make sure capitalization, punctuation, and spelling are correct.

Copy your revised draft on the lines below.

_____

_____

_____

_____

_____

_____

_____

_____

_____

Read your final draft out loud, and touch each word as you read. Correct all capitalization, punctuation, and spelling errors.

☐ **Corrected capitalization errors**

☐ **Corrected punctuation errors**

☐ **Corrected spelling errors**

Expository Paragraph
Checklist

Indent and Opening Sentence

- [ ] Did you indent your opening sentence?
- [ ] Did you write an opening sentence?
- [ ] Does your opening sentence introduce the topic?

Body Sentences

- [ ] Did you write three or more body sentences?
- [ ] Does each sentence begin with a different word?
- [ ] Did you stay on topic?

Closing Sentence

- [ ] Did you write a closing sentence?
- [ ] Does the closing sentence end your topic?

Overall

- [ ] Did you use descriptive adjectives?
- [ ] Did you use descriptive action verbs?
- [ ] Did you use descriptive adverbs (when appropriate)?

Mechanics

- [ ] Did you check your spelling?
- [ ] Did you use capitalization correctly?
- [ ] Did you use punctuation correctly?

EXTRA PRACTICE
Expository Paragraph

Now it's your turn!

1. Read the **prompt**. Then, **brainstorm** your ideas <u>on a clean sheet of paper</u> and choose a topic.

If you could travel anywhere in the world, where would you go? In a paragraph, explain where you would go and why you want to go there.

2. **Plan** and **organize** your thoughts using **graphic organizer(s)**. (Additional graphic organizers available in the *Assessment/Resource Booklet*)

3. **Draft** your paragraph on a clean sheet of paper using the information in your plan.

4. **Revise** your draft. Start by reading your draft out loud, <u>touching each word as you read</u>. Search for way to add or change words, phrases, or sentences to improve your writing.

<u>CHECKLIST</u>

☐ Revised words
☐ Revised sentences

5. **Edit** and **publish** your **final draft**. Copy your revised draft to a clean sheet of paper. Correct all capitalization, punctuation, and spelling errors.

<u>CHECKLIST</u>

☐ Corrected capitalization errors
☐ Corrected punctuation errors
☐ Corrected spelling errors

Lesson 49 – Expository Personal Letter

A *personal letter* is a letter you write to family or friends. A letter has five main parts: *date, greeting, body, closing,* and *signature.*

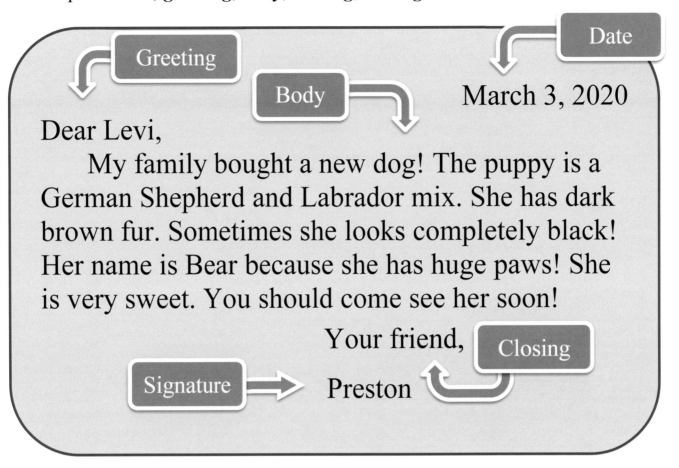

A *personal letter* has five parts: **date, greeting, body, closing,** and **signature.**

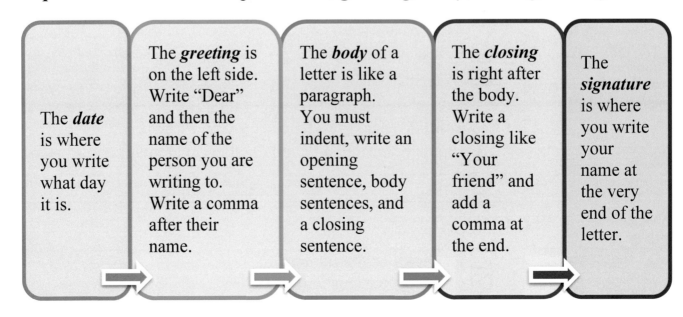

Lesson 49 – Expository Personal Letter
Brainstorm

Expository writing explains, describes, or informs.
A *personal letter* is a letter you write to family or friends.

 Brainstorm to choose a topic. Write down many ideas. Narrow the ideas down, then choose one idea to be your topic.

Prompt

- *If you could spend a whole day with someone special, who would it be? Write a personal letter to someone who is special to you. Explain what you would like to do if you could spend an entire day with them.*

First, list many people you would choose to spend a whole day with.

Next, choose three people from the list and record them in the boxes below.

Finally, draw a line through two people and record your final choice in the box below.

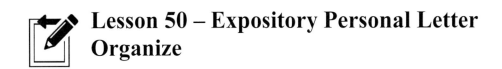

Lesson 50 – Expository Personal Letter
Organize

Make a plan for an *opening sentence, body sentences,* and a *closing sentence* for the body of your personal letter.

Use the graphic organizer to plan your letter about your topic.

Write ideas for the beginning of your letter. Write what your topic is.

Opening >

Write ideas for the middle of your letter. Write details about your topic.

Detail >

Detail >

Detail >

Write ideas for the end of your letter. Close your topic.

Closing >

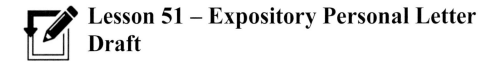 **Lesson 51 – Expository Personal Letter**
Draft

In a draft, take the ideas from your plan and make them complete sentences.

At this step of the writing process, your writing does not have to be perfect. Instead, try to make your ideas clear.

Draft your personal letter. Use the ideas from your plan.

_____

_____

_____

_____

_____

_____

_____

_____

_____

_____

_____

_____

Lesson 52 – Expository Personal Letter Revise

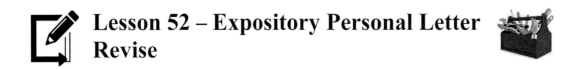

Look for ways to add descriptive adjectives and action verbs to your writing. If your sentences all begin with the same word, look for ways to use different beginning words.

Remember, you do not have to change *everything* you have written. Only make changes that **improve** your writing.

> **Draft**
> *I would have a great time.*

> **Revised**
> ***Overall, spending an entire day with you would be very special.***

Revise your draft. Read your draft out loud, and touch each word as you read. Look for ways to add or change details, words, or sentences.

- Reading out loud will help you notice details you do not see when you read silently.
- Touching each word will help you focus on one thing at a time.

Read your draft out loud, and touch each word as you read.

☐ **Revised words**

☐ **Revised sentences**

164

Lesson 53 – Expository Personal Letter
Final Draft

Make a **copy** of your revised draft on a new piece of paper. **Edit** your writing to make sure capitalization, punctuation, and spelling are correct.

Copy your revised draft on the lines below.

_____

_____

_____

_____

_____

_____

_____

_____

_____

_____

_____

Read your final draft out loud, and touch each word as you read. Correct all capitalization, punctuation, and spelling errors.

☐ **Corrected capitalization errors**

☐ **Corrected punctuation errors**

☐ **Corrected spelling errors**

Expository Personal Letter Checklist

Indent and Opening Sentence

- [ ] Did you indent your opening sentence?
- [ ] Did you write an opening sentence?
- [ ] Does your opening sentence introduce the topic?

Body Sentences

- [ ] Did you write three or more body sentences?
- [ ] Does each sentence begin with a different word?
- [ ] Did you stay on topic?

Closing Sentence

- [ ] Did you write a closing sentence?
- [ ] Does the closing sentence end your topic?

Overall

- [ ] Did you use descriptive adjectives?
- [ ] Did you use descriptive action verbs?
- [ ] Did you use descriptive adverbs (when appropriate)?

Mechanics

- [ ] Did you check your spelling?
- [ ] Did you use capitalization correctly?
- [ ] Did you use punctuation correctly?
- [ ] Did you include all parts of a letter? (Checklist on next page)

Expository Personal Letter Checklist

Date

- [ ] Is the date in the upper right-hand side of the paper?
- [ ] Is the month capitalized?
- [ ] Is there a comma between the day and the year?

Greeting

- [ ] Is "Dear" capitalized?
- [ ] Is the person's name capitalized?
- [ ] Did you write a comma after the person's name?

Closing

- [ ] Did you write the closing below the body, in the middle of the page?
- [ ] Did you capitalize the first word of the closing?
- [ ] Did you write a comma after the closing?

Signature

- [ ] Is your signature lined up with the closing?
- [ ] Did you capitalize your signature?

EXTRA PRACTICE
Expository Personal Letter

Now it's your turn!

1. Read the **prompt**. Then, **brainstorm** your ideas <u>on a clean sheet of paper</u> and choose a topic.

Think of a game you would like to play with your friend. It could be a board game, a video game, or another kind of game. Write a personal letter to your friend. Explain what the game is and why you want to play it with them.

2. **Plan** and **organize** your thoughts using **graphic organizer(s)**. (Additional graphic organizers available in the *Assessment/Resource Booklet*)

3. **Draft** your letter on a clean sheet of paper using the information in your plan.

4. **Revise** your draft. Start by reading your draft out loud, <u>touching each word as you read</u>. Search for way to add or change words, phrases, or sentences to improve your writing.

<u>**CHECKLIST**</u>

☐ Revised words
☐ Revised sentences

5. Edit and **publish** your **final draft**. Copy your revised draft to a clean sheet of paper. Correct all capitalization, punctuation, and spelling errors.

<u>**CHECKLIST**</u>

☐ Corrected capitalization errors
☐ Corrected punctuation errors
☐ Corrected spelling errors

STOP Complete Assessment 17

Lesson 54 – Persuasive Paragraph

Persuasive writing tries to convince a reader using facts and examples to support an opinion.

Persuasion usually takes one of two forms.

1 The writer wants the reader to believe or not to believe something.

2 The writer wants the reader to do or not to do something.

Look at this example of a *persuasive paragraph*. This paragraph is answering the prompt: *Should dogs be allowed on city sidewalks? Persuade your reader to agree with your opinion.*

The opening sentence reveals the writer's *persuasive opinion*.

Dogs should be allowed on city sidewalks. Dogs need exercise. If dogs are not allowed on the sidewalk, they will have to walk in the street. That is dangerous! Also, a friendly dog on the sidewalk will make people happy. Dogs should be allowed to walk on sidewalks with their owners.

The details *support* the persuasive opinion with facts and examples.

Lesson 54 – Persuasive Paragraph Brainstorm

Persuasive writing tries to convince a reader using facts and examples to support an opinion.

 Brainstorm to choose a topic. Write down many ideas. Narrow the ideas down, then choose one idea to be your topic.

Prompt

• *Think of your favorite food. Imagine that you meet someone who has never eaten it before. Write a persuasive paragraph to convince the person that they should try it.*

Based on the prompt, what is your purpose for writing this persuasive paragraph?

☐ To convince the reader to believe or not to believe something.

☐ To convince the reader to do or not to do something.

First, list many different foods to choose from.

Next, choose three foods from the list and record them in the boxes below.

Finally, draw a line through two foods and record your final choice in the box below.

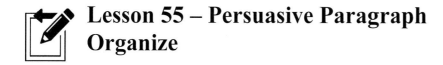

Lesson 55 – Persuasive Paragraph
Organize

Make a plan for an *opening sentence, body sentences,* and a *closing sentence.*

Use the graphic organizer to plan your paragraph about your topic.

Write ideas for the beginning of your paragraph. Write what your persuasive opinion is.

Opening

Write ideas for the middle of your paragraph. Write support for your persuasive opinion.

Detail

Detail

Detail

Write ideas for the end of your paragraph. Close your persuasive argument.

Closing

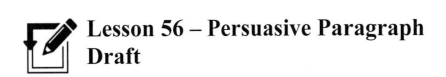 **Lesson 56 – Persuasive Paragraph Draft**

In a draft, take the ideas from your plan and make them complete sentences.

At this step of the writing process, your writing does not have to be perfect. Instead, try to make your ideas clear.

Draft your paragraph. Use the ideas from your plan.

_____

_____

_____

_____

_____

_____

_____

_____

_____

_____

_____

Lesson 57 – Persuasive Paragraph Revise

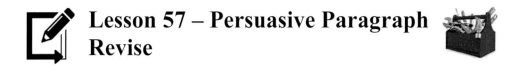

Look for ways to add descriptive adjectives and action verbs to your writing. If your sentences all begin with the same word, look for ways to use different beginning words.

Remember, you do not have to change *everything* you have written. Only make changes that **improve** your writing.

> **Draft**
> *It is made from fruit. It is healthy.*

> **Revised**
> ***Blueberry pie is made from fruit, so it is healthy.***

Revise your draft. Read your draft out loud, and touch each word as you read. Look for ways to add or change details, words, or sentences.

- Reading out loud will help you notice details you do not see when you read silently.
- Touching each word will help you focus on one thing at a time.

Read your draft out loud, and touch each word as you read.

☐   **Revised words**

☐   **Revised sentences**

Lesson 58 – Persuasive Paragraph
Final Draft

Make a **copy** of your revised draft on a new piece of paper. **Edit** your writing to make sure capitalization, punctuation, and spelling are correct.

Copy your revised draft on the lines below.

_____

_____

_____

_____

_____

_____

_____

_____

_____

Read your final draft out loud, and touch each word as you read. Correct all capitalization, punctuation, and spelling errors.

☐ **Corrected capitalization errors**

☐ **Corrected punctuation errors**

☐ **Corrected spelling errors**

Persuasive Paragraph
Checklist

Indent and Opening Sentence

☐ Did you indent your opening sentence?

☐ Did you write an opening sentence?

☐ Does your opening sentence introduce your persuasive opinion?

Body Sentences

☐ Did you write three or more body sentences?

☐ Do your body sentences include details that support your opinion?

☐ Does each sentence begin with a different word?

☐ Did you stay on topic?

Closing Sentence

☐ Did you write a closing sentence?

☐ Does the closing sentence end your topic?

Overall

☐ Did you use descriptive adjectives?

☐ Did you use descriptive action verbs?

☐ Did you use descriptive adverbs (when appropriate)?

Mechanics

☐ Did you check your spelling?

☐ Did you use capitalization correctly?

☐ Did you use punctuation correctly?

EXTRA PRACTICE
Persuasive Paragraph

Now it's your turn!

1. Read the **prompt**. Then, **brainstorm** your ideas <u>on a clean sheet of paper</u> and choose a topic.

Are vacations to the beach better than vacations to the mountains? In a paragraph, persuade the reader to agree with your opinion. Use many details that support your argument.

2. **Plan** and **organize** your thoughts using **graphic organizer(s)**. (Additional graphic organizers available in the *Assessment/Resource Booklet*)

3. **Draft** your paragraph on a clean sheet of paper using the information in your plan.

4. **Revise** your draft. Start by reading your draft out loud, <u>touching each word as you read</u>. Search for way to add or change words, phrases, or sentences to improve your writing.

CHECKLIST

☐ Revised words
☐ Revised sentences

5. **Edit** and **publish** your **final draft**. Copy your revised draft to a clean sheet of paper. Correct all capitalization, punctuation, and spelling errors.

CHECKLIST

☐ Corrected capitalization errors
☐ Corrected punctuation errors
☐ Corrected spelling errors

Lesson 59 – Persuasive Personal Letter

A *persuasive personal letter* is a letter written to friends or family to convince them using facts and examples to support an opinion.

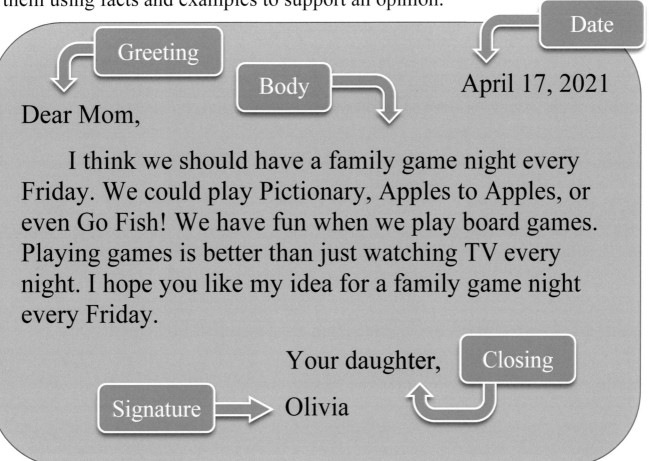

A *personal letter* has five parts: **date, greeting, body, closing,** and **signature.**

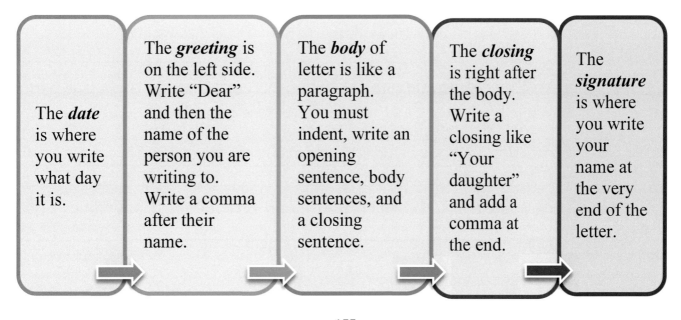

Lesson 59 – Persuasive Personal Letter
Brainstorm

Persuasive writing tries to convince a reader using facts and examples to support an opinion.

A ***personal letter*** is a letter you write to family or friends. A letter has five main parts: ***date, greeting, body, closing,*** and ***signature.***

 Brainstorm to choose a topic. Write down many ideas. Narrow the ideas down, then choose one idea to be your topic.

Prompt

- *Pretend you and your best friend want to go to a costume party together. What costumes should you and your friend wear? Write a letter to your friend and convince them to agree with your costume idea.*

First, list many different costume ideas for you and your friend.

Next, choose three costumes from the list and record them in the boxes below.

Finally, draw a line through two costumes and record your final choice in the box below.

Lesson 60 – Persuasive Personal Letter
Organize

Make a plan for an *opening sentence, body sentences,* and a *closing sentence* for the body of your personal letter.

Use the graphic organizer to plan your letter about your topic.

Write ideas for the beginning of your letter. Write what your persuasive topic is.

Opening

Write ideas for the middle of your letter. Write support for your persuasive topic.

Detail

Detail

Detail

Write ideas for the end of your letter. Close your persuasive topic.

Closing

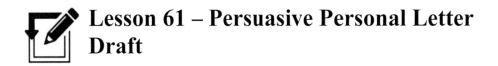 **Lesson 61 – Persuasive Personal Letter Draft**

In a draft, take the ideas from your plan and make them complete sentences.

At this step of the writing process, your writing does not have to be perfect. Instead, try to make your ideas clear.

Draft your personal letter. Use the ideas from your plan.

_____

_____

_____

_____

_____

_____

_____

_____

_____

_____

_____

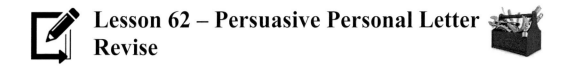

Lesson 62 – Persuasive Personal Letter Revise

Look for ways to add descriptive adjectives and action verbs to your writing. If your sentences all begin with the same word, look for ways to use different beginning words.

Remember, you do not have to change *everything* you have written. Only make changes that **improve** your writing.

> **Draft**
> *We are the right height. We are male and female.*

> **Revised**
> ***We are the right height, and we are male and female.***

Revise your draft. Read your draft out loud, and touch each word as you read. Look for ways to add or change details, words, or sentences.

- Reading out loud will help you notice details you do not see when you read silently.
- Touching each word will help you focus on one thing at a time.

Read your draft out loud, and touch each word as you read.

☐ **Revised words**

☐ **Revised sentences**

Lesson 63 – Persuasive Personal Letter
Final Draft

Make a **copy** of your revised draft on a new piece of paper. **Edit** your writing to make sure capitalization, punctuation, and spelling are correct.

Copy your revised draft on the lines below.

_____

_____

_____

_____

_____

_____

_____

_____

_____

_____

Read your final draft out loud, and touch each word as you read. Correct all capitalization, punctuation, and spelling errors.

☐ **Corrected capitalization errors**

☐ **Corrected punctuation errors**

☐ **Corrected spelling errors**

Persuasive Personal Letter Checklist

Indent and Opening Sentence

- [ ] Did you indent your opening sentence?
- [ ] Did you write an opening sentence?
- [ ] Does your opening sentence introduce your persuasive opinion?

Body Sentences

- [ ] Did you write three or more body sentences?
- [ ] Do your body sentences include details that support your opinion?
- [ ] Does each sentence begin with a different word?
- [ ] Did you stay on topic?

Closing Sentence

- [ ] Did you write a closing sentence?
- [ ] Does the closing sentence end your topic?

Overall

- [ ] Did you use descriptive adjectives?
- [ ] Did you use descriptive action verbs?
- [ ] Did you use descriptive adverbs (when appropriate)?

Mechanics

- [ ] Did you check your spelling?
- [ ] Did you use capitalization correctly?
- [ ] Did you use punctuation correctly?
- [ ] Did you include all parts of a letter? (Checklist on next page)

Persuasive Personal Letter
Format Checklist

Date

☐ Is the date in the upper right-hand side of the paper?

☐ Is the month capitalized?

☐ Is there a comma between the day and the year?

Greeting

☐ Is "Dear" capitalized?

☐ Is the person's name capitalized?

☐ Did you write a comma after the person's name?

Closing

☐ Did you write the closing below the body, in the middle of the page?

☐ Did you capitalize the first word of the closing?

☐ Did you write a comma after the closing?

Signature

☐ Is your signature lined up with the closing?

☐ Did you capitalize your signature?

EXTRA PRACTICE
Persuasive Personal Letter

Now it's your turn!

1. Read the **prompt**. Then, **brainstorm** your ideas <u>on a clean sheet of paper</u> and choose a topic.

Pretend that you want to start a business with your friend. The business could be making things, selling things, or helping people by performing a service. Write a personal letter to your friend. Persuade them to join your business idea.

2. **Plan** and **organize** your thoughts using **graphic organizer(s)**. (Additional graphic organizers available in the *Assessment/Resource Booklet*)

3. **Draft** your letter on a clean sheet of paper using the information in your plan.

4. **Revise** your draft. Start by reading your draft out loud, <u>touching each word as you read</u>. Search for way to add or change words, phrases, or sentences to improve your writing.

CHECKLIST

☐ Revised words
☐ Revised sentences

5. **Edit** and **publish** your **final draft**. Copy your revised draft to a clean sheet of paper. Correct all capitalization, punctuation, and spelling errors.

CHECKLIST

☐ Corrected capitalization errors
☐ Corrected punctuation errors
☐ Corrected spelling errors

185

STOP **Complete Assessment 18**

Lesson 64 – Descriptive Paragraph

Descriptive writing describes someone or something using sensory details.

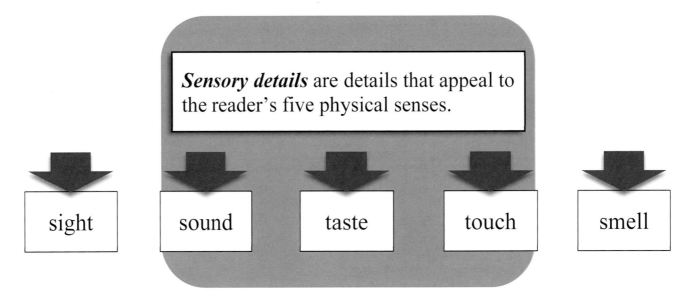

Look at this example of a *descriptive paragraph*. This paragraph is answering the prompt: *What is it like to sleep during a thunderstorm? Describe what it would be like to sleep during a storm.*

The opening sentence introduces the writer's descriptive topic.

Sleeping during a thunderstorm is hard! The thunder is loud and shakes the windows. I put my head under my pillow, but I can still hear it. The lightning is so bright! It is like the lights that are in my room. Rain hits my windows with a loud clattering sound. I can't get any sleep during a storm!

The details *describe* the topic with *sensory details*.

Lesson 64 – Descriptive Paragraph
Brainstorm

Descriptive writing describes someone or something using sensory details.

 Brainstorm to choose a topic. Write down many ideas. Narrow the ideas down, then choose one idea to be your topic.

Prompt

• *Imagine that when you woke up, you discovered that a foot of snow fell overnight. In a paragraph, describe what you see out of your bedroom window. Remember to use sensory details.*

Based on the prompt, what do you imagine you will be able to see? Can you imagine feeling or hearing anything as well? Record your ideas in the box below. If you want, you can also draw a picture of what you imagine.

What physical senses do your ideas appeal to?

sight   sound   taste   touch   smell

Lesson 65 – Descriptive Paragraph
Organize

Make a plan for an *opening sentence, body sentences,* and a *closing sentence.*

Remember to include *sensory details!*

Use the graphic organizer to plan your paragraph about your topic.

Write ideas for the beginning of your paragraph. Write what your topic is.

Opening

Write ideas for the middle of your paragraph. Write details about your topic.

Detail

Detail

Detail

Write ideas for the end of your paragraph. Close your topic.

Closing

 **Lesson 66 – Descriptive Paragraph**
Draft

In a draft, take the ideas from your plan and make them complete sentences.

At the step of the writing process, your writing does not have to be perfect. Instead, try to make your ideas clear.

Draft your paragraph. Use the ideas from your plan.

_____

_____

_____

_____

_____

_____

_____

_____

_____

_____

_____

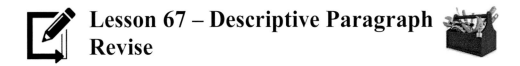

Lesson 67 – Descriptive Paragraph Revise

Look for ways to add descriptive adjectives and action verbs to your writing. If your sentences all begin with the same word, look for ways to use different beginning words.

Remember, you do not have to change *everything* you have written. Only make changes that **improve** your writing.

> **Draft**
> *In my backyard, I couldn't see anything.*

> **Revised**
> ***In my backyard, a blanket of snow covered everything, and I couldn't see anything.***

Revise your draft. Read your draft out loud, and touch each word as you read. Look for ways to add or change details, words, or sentences.

- Reading out loud will help you notice details you do not see when you read silently.
- Touching each word will help you focus on one thing at a time.

Read your draft out loud, and touch each word as you read.

☐ **Revised words**

☐ **Revised sentences**

Circle the kinds of *sensory details* that you included in your paragraph.

SIGHT   SOUND   TASTE   TOUCH   SMELL

Lesson 68 – Descriptive Paragraph
Final Draft

Make a **copy** of your revised draft on a new piece of paper. **Edit** your writing to make sure capitalization, punctuation, and spelling are correct.

Copy your revised draft on the lines below.

_____

_____

_____

_____

_____

_____

_____

_____

_____

_____

Read your final draft out loud, and touch each word as you read. Correct all capitalization, punctuation, and spelling errors.

☐ **Corrected capitalization errors**
☐ **Corrected punctuation errors**
☐ **Corrected spelling errors**

Descriptive Paragraph Checklist

Indent and Opening Sentence

- [ ] Did you indent your opening sentence?
- [ ] Did you write an opening sentence?
- [ ] Does your opening sentence introduce the topic?

Body Sentences

- [ ] Did you write three or more body sentences?
- [ ] Do your body sentences include sensory details?
- [ ] Does each sentence begin with a different word?
- [ ] Did you stay on topic?

Closing Sentence

- [ ] Did you write a closing sentence?
- [ ] Does the closing sentence end your topic?

Overall

- [ ] Did you use descriptive adjectives?
- [ ] Did you use descriptive action verbs?
- [ ] Did you use descriptive adverbs (when appropriate)?

Mechanics

- [ ] Did you check your spelling?
- [ ] Did you use capitalization correctly?
- [ ] Did you use punctuation correctly?

EXTRA PRACTICE
Descriptive Paragraph

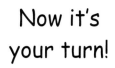 

Now it's your turn!

1. Read the **prompt**. Then, **brainstorm** your ideas <u>on a clean sheet of paper</u> and choose a topic.

Imagine that you turned into an animal for one day. Describe the world from the point of view of the animal. Use sensory details in your description.

2. **Plan** and **organize** your thoughts using **graphic organizer(s)**. (Additional graphic organizers available in the *Assessment/Resource Booklet*)

3. **Draft** your paragraph on a clean sheet of paper using the information in your plan.

4. **Revise** your draft. Start by reading your draft out loud, <u>touching each word as you read</u>. Search for way to add or change words, phrases, or sentences to improve your writing.

CHECKLIST

- ☐ Revised words
- ☐ Revised sentences

5. **Edit** and **publish** your **final draft**. Copy your revised draft to a clean sheet of paper. Correct all capitalization, punctuation, and spelling errors.

CHECKLIST

- ☐ Corrected capitalization errors
- ☐ Corrected punctuation errors
- ☐ Corrected spelling errors

Lesson 69 – Imaginative Narrative

An *imaginative narrative* is an imagined or make-believe story about a series of events.

An *imaginative narrative*
- focuses on a *single story*
- has a *hook*, *events*, a *climax*, and a *closing*
- is told in *chronological order*
- uses *transitions*

> Imaginative narratives use *sensory details.* Sensory details appeal to the reader's five physical senses: *sight, sound, taste, touch, smell.*

Hook

Transition

I woke up one morning at the bottom of the ocean. At first, I was scared. Then I wanted to explore! First, I swam with rainbow fish. Their scales were shimmery and bright. The water was cold, but swimming was fun! Next, I saw an octopus with bright lights on its tentacles. It waved to me! Finally, I found a dark cave. A family of giant red crabs lived there. I tried to make friends with them, but they tried to eat me! I swam away as fast as I could. After that, I was done exploring. I swam back to the beach and went home.

Events

Climax

Closing

The **hook** grabs the reader's attention and introduces the narrative.	The **events** are written in **chronological order**. Events in a narrative are written with **sensory details**.	The **climax** of a narrative is the most exciting event. The climax is made up of a **problem** and a **solution**.	The **closing** ends the narrative.

Lesson 69 – Imaginative Narrative
Chronological Order and Transitions

An ***imaginative narrative*** is an imagined or make-believe story about a series of events. A narrative is always told in ***chronological order***. ***Transitions*** are words that help show the order of events.

When a story is told in ***chronological order***, the events are described in the same order that they happened.

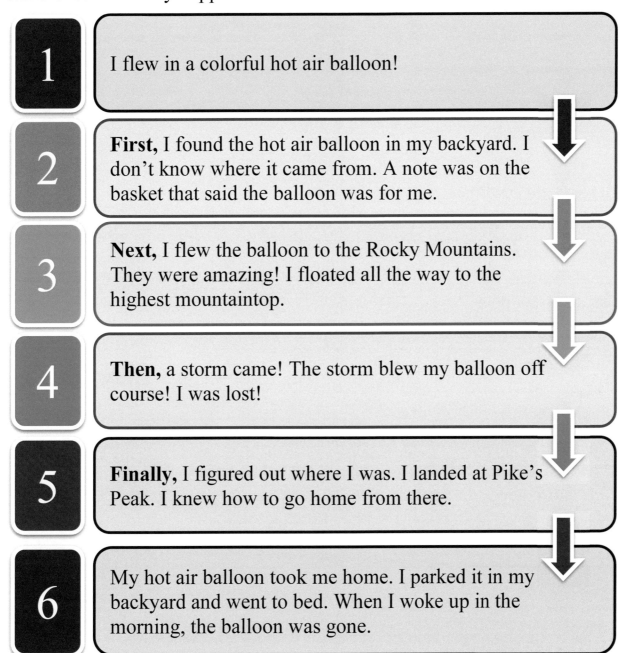

1   I flew in a colorful hot air balloon!

2   **First,** I found the hot air balloon in my backyard. I don't know where it came from. A note was on the basket that said the balloon was for me.

3   **Next,** I flew the balloon to the Rocky Mountains. They were amazing! I floated all the way to the highest mountaintop.

4   **Then,** a storm came! The storm blew my balloon off course! I was lost!

5   **Finally,** I figured out where I was. I landed at Pike's Peak. I knew how to go home from there.

6   My hot air balloon took me home. I parked it in my backyard and went to bed. When I woke up in the morning, the balloon was gone.

Lesson 69 – Imaginative Narrative
Chronological Order and Transitions

When a story is told in *chronological order*, the events are described in the same order that they happened.

Transitions are words that help show the order of events.

Write a *transition* in the boxes to accurately show time and the *chronological order* of events.

	Common Transitions

[   ] , my friends and I found an abandoned fort in the woods.

[   ] , we chose to make the fort our own secret hideout.

First

[   ] , a black bear came out the front door!

Next

[   ] , we screamed and ran all the way back home.

Then

Read the statement below. Add a *transition* and second event.

Finally

First, my father brought home a cardboard box.

[   ] , _____

After

_____

_____

Lesson 70 – Imaginative Narrative Brainstorm

An *imaginative narrative* is an imagined or make-believe story about a series of events. An *imaginative narrative*

- focuses on a *single story*
- has a *hook*, *events*, a *climax*, and a *closing*
- is told in *chronological order*
- uses *transitions*

 Brainstorm to choose a topic. Write down many ideas. Narrow the ideas down, then choose one idea to be your topic.

Prompt

- *Write an imaginative narrative that describes an exciting adventure. Tell the story of the adventure. Remember to use sensory details!*

First, list many different exciting adventures.

Next, choose three adventures from the list. Record them in the boxes below.

Finally, draw a line through two adventures. Record your final choice in the box below.

 **Lesson 70 – Imaginative Narrative**
Organize

Make a plan for the *hook, events, climax,* and *closing* of your imaginative narrative.

Use the graphic organizer to plan your narrative about your topic.

Hook

Event

Event

Climax

Problem

Solution

Closing

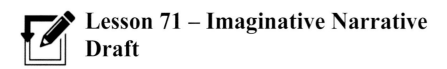

Lesson 71 – Imaginative Narrative
Draft

In a draft, take the ideas from your plan and make them complete sentences. At this step of the writing process, your writing does not have to be perfect. Instead, try to make your ideas clear.

Remember to use *transitions* between the events of your imaginative narrative.

Common Transitions				
First	Next	Then	Finally	After

Draft your narrative. Use the ideas from your plan.

_____

_____

_____

_____

_____

_____

_____

_____

_____

More space to write on next page →

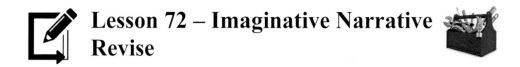

Lesson 72 – Imaginative Narrative Revise

Look for ways to add descriptive adjectives and action verbs to your writing. If your sentences all begin with the same word, look for ways to use different beginning words.

Remember, you do not have to change *everything* you have written. Only make changes that *improve* your writing.

Draft
As home got little, I could see outer space getting near.

Revised
As home disappeared behind me, I could see outer space getting near.

Revise your draft. Read your draft out loud, and touch each word as you read. Look for ways to add or change details, words, or sentences.

- Reading out loud will help you notice details you do not see when you read silently.
- Touching each word will help you focus on one thing at a time.

Read your draft out loud, and touch each word as you read.

☐   **Revised words**

☐   **Revised sentences**

Circle the kinds of *sensory details* that you included in your narrative.

SIGHT   SOUND   TASTE   TOUCH   SMELL

Lesson 73 – Imaginative Narrative
Final Draft

Make a **copy** of your revised draft on a new piece of paper. **Edit** your writing to make sure capitalization, punctuation, and spelling are correct.

Copy your revised draft on the lines below.

_____

_____

_____

_____

_____

_____

_____

_____

_____

_____

_____

More space to write on next page →

_____

_____

_____

_____

_____

_____

_____

_____

_____

_____

_____

_____

Read your final draft out loud, and touch each word as you read. Correct all capitalization, punctuation, and spelling errors.

☐ **Corrected capitalization errors**

☐ **Corrected punctuation errors**

☐ **Corrected spelling errors**

Imaginative Narrative Checklist

Indent and Opening Sentence

- [ ] Did you indent your opening sentence?
- [ ] Does your opening sentence introduce the topic?
- [ ] Does your opening sentence grab the reader's attention?

Body Sentences

- [ ] Did you write at least two events and a climax?
- [ ] Are the events in chronological order?
- [ ] Did you include at least three transitions?
- [ ] Does each sentence begin with a different word?

Closing Sentence

- [ ] Does the closing sentence end your topic?

Overall

- [ ] Did you use descriptive adjectives, action verbs, and adverbs (when appropriate)?
- [ ] Do you have a clear beginning, middle, and end?
- [ ] Did you include sensory details?

Mechanics

- [ ] Did you check your spelling?
- [ ] Did you use capitalization correctly?
- [ ] Did you use punctuation correctly?

EXTRA PRACTICE

Imaginative Narrative

Now it's your turn!

1. Read the **prompt**. Then, **brainstorm** your ideas <u>on a clean sheet of paper</u> and choose a topic.

Imagine taking a fun trip. It could be a vacation, a field trip, or another kind of fun trip. What would happen on this trip? What problems would you face? How would you overcome these problems? Write an imaginative narrative and tell the story of the trip. Remember to use sensory details!

2. **Plan** and **organize** your thoughts using **graphic organizer(s)**.
(Additional graphic organizers available in the *Assessment/Resource Booklet*)

3. **Draft** your imaginative narrative on a clean sheet of paper using the information in your plan.

4. **Revise** your draft. Start by reading your draft out loud, <u>touching each word as you read</u>. Search for way to add or change words, phrases, or sentences to improve your writing.

CHECKLIST

☐ Revised words
☐ Revised sentences

5. **Edit** and **publish** your **final draft**. Copy your revised draft to a clean sheet of paper. Correct all capitalization, punctuation, and spelling errors.

CHECKLIST

☐ Corrected capitalization errors
☐ Corrected punctuation errors
☐ Corrected spelling errors

STOP **Complete Assessment 19**

Lesson 74 – Research Project
Process

The *research process* is similar to the *writing process*. The research process has six steps: *brainstorm, research, organize, draft, revise,* and *final draft.*

BRAINSTORM

First, choose a topic.

RESEARCH

Second, gather information from books, magazines, and websites.

ORGANIZE

Third, make a plan.

DRAFT

Fourth, put your ideas in order.

REVISE

Fifth, revise your draft

FINAL DRAFT

Sixth, edit your work and create a final copy.

Lesson 74 – Research Project Process

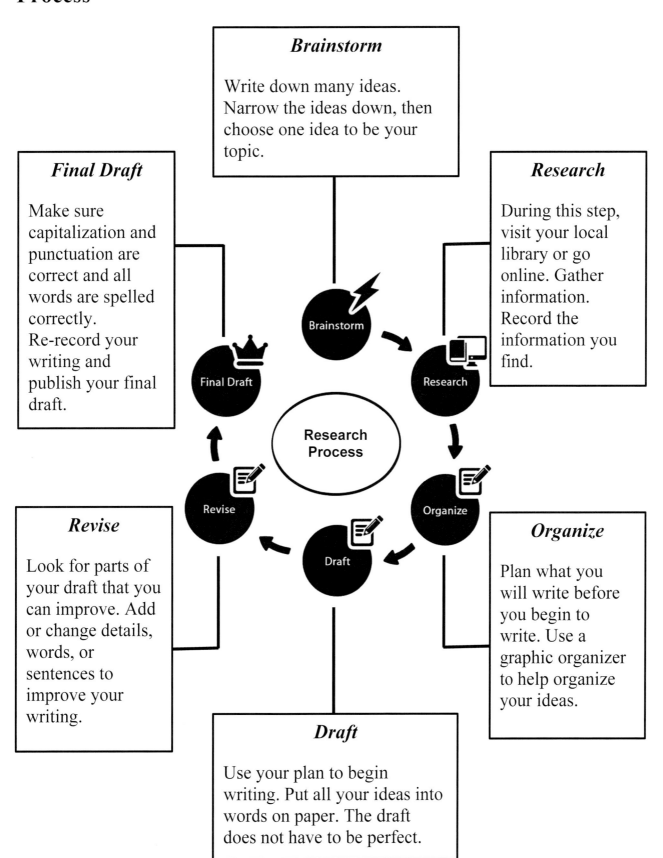

Brainstorm

Write down many ideas. Narrow the ideas down, then choose one idea to be your topic.

Research

During this step, visit your local library or go online. Gather information. Record the information you find.

Final Draft

Make sure capitalization and punctuation are correct and all words are spelled correctly. Re-record your writing and publish your final draft.

Revise

Look for parts of your draft that you can improve. Add or change details, words, or sentences to improve your writing.

Organize

Plan what you will write before you begin to write. Use a graphic organizer to help organize your ideas.

Draft

Use your plan to begin writing. Put all your ideas into words on paper. The draft does not have to be perfect.

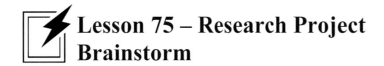
Lesson 75 – Research Project
Brainstorm

In a ***research project***, you gather information to share with your audience. You can share the information in a long writing assignment or in a visual presentation.

In this research project, you will create a ***visual presentation*** that includes words and pictures. You will share information on a ***display board***.

 Brainstorm to choose a topic. Write down many ideas. Narrow the ideas down, then choose one idea to be your topic.

Prompt

- *What do you know about your state/province? Research the history of your state/province. What important events happened there? Who is an important person from your state/province? What kind of animals and plants are in the region? Share your research in a visual presentation that includes pictures and organized paragraphs.*

 In some cases, your topic is given to you by the prompt. In these special circumstances, it is unnecessary to brainstorm a topic. Instead, this step can be skipped, and you can move straight into the next writing stage!

You do not need to brainstorm for a topic of this research project. Instead, record the name of your state/province in the space provided, and move straight to the research step of the research process.

What is the name of your state/province?

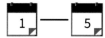

 **Lesson 76 – Research Project**
Gather Information

Before you begin creating your research project, you must gather information about your state/province. This is the second step in the research process.

RESEARCH

- *Gather information from books, magazines, and websites.* Record the information you find.

The worksheets in the this lesson will help you know what information to look for. The information will come from books and magazines, the internet, or from interviews with people who know about the topic.

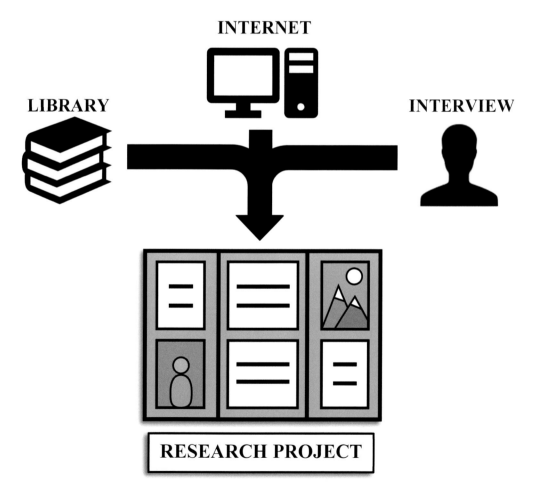

After you gather important information, you will use this information to create your research project.

Lesson 76 – Research Project
Gather Information

Before you begin creating your research project, you must gather information about your state/province. The worksheets in the this lesson will help you know what information to look for. The information will come from books and magazines, the internet, or from interviews with people who know about the topic.

What is the name of your state/province?

RESEARCH

Go to the library. Use the following sources to gather information:

- books
- magazines
- internet websites
- other quality sources

Gather information to answer these research questions:

1. What is your state/province?
2. What important event happened in your state/province?
3. Who is an important person from your state/province?
4. What kinds of plants and animals are in your state/province?

Use the worksheets on the following pages to help guide you to find pictures and information to use in your project. *This step could take several days.*

Read ⟩ Choose quality sources ⟩ Complete research ⟩ Document sources

Lesson 76 – Research Project
Gather Information – Topic #1

You will use this information on page 220.

Your state/province: _____

Record information from your sources to answer the research questions for your first topic. Remember to use your own words. Do not copy the words from your sources exactly.

Topic #1: What is your state/province?

- **Where is your state/province?**

- **When was your state/province founded?**

- **What is the nickname of your state/province?**

Where did you find the information? _____

_____

Lesson 76 – Research Project
Gather Information – Topic #1

Your state/province: _____

Find at least two pictures that are connected to your first research topic. Attach the pictures to the spaces provided. Consider the research questions on the previous page to help guide you to find pictures. *Note: You will need two copies of each picture you choose: one to paste to this page and one to use in your final project.*

DO NOT USE PICTURES THAT ARE COPYRIGHTED.

A picture of a map of your
state/province

A picture of a nice place in
your state/province

Where did you find the information? _____

Lesson 76 – Research Project
Gather Information – Topic #2

You will use this information on page 221.

Your state/province: _____

Record information from your sources to answer the research questions for your second topic. Remember to use your own words. Do not copy the words from your sources exactly.

Topic #2: What important event happened in your state/province?

- **What happened?**

- **When did it happen?**

- **Where in the state/province did it happen?**

Where did you find the information? _____

_____

 **Lesson 76 – Research Project**
Gather Information –Topic #2

Your state/province: _____

Find at least two pictures that are connected to your second research topic. Attach the pictures to the spaces provided. Consider the research questions on the previous page to help guide you to find pictures. *Note: You will need two copies of each picture you choose: one to paste to this page and one to use in your final project.*

DO NOT USE PICTURES THAT ARE COPYRIGHTED.

A picture or illustration of
an important event in the
history of your
state/province

A picture of a statue or
other object that helps
people remember the event

Where did you find the information? _____

Lesson 76 – Research Project
Gather Information – Topic #3

You will use this information on page 222.

Your state/province: _____

Record information from your sources to answer the research questions for your third topic. Remember to use your own words. Do not copy the words from your sources exactly.

Topic #3: Who is an important person from your state/province?

- **What is their name?**

- **When were they born?**

- **What important thing did they do?**

Where did you find the information? _____
_____

215

Lesson 76 – Research Project
Gather Information – Topic #3

Your state/province: _____

Find at least two pictures that are connected to your third research topic. Attach the pictures to the spaces provided. Consider the research questions on the previous page to help guide you to find pictures. *Note: You will need two copies of each picture you choose: one to paste to this page and one to use in your final project.*

DO NOT USE PICTURES THAT ARE COPYRIGHTED.

A picture or illustration of an important person from your state/province

Another picture or illustration of an important person from your state/province

Where did you find the information? _____

Lesson 76 – Research Project
Gather Information – Topic #4

You will use this information on page **223**.

Your state/province: _____

Record information from your sources to answer the research questions for your fourth topic. Remember to use your own words. Do not copy the words from your sources exactly.

Topic #4: What kinds of plants and animals are in your state/province?

- **What is a common plant in your state/province?**

- **What is the plant like?**

- **What is a common animal in your state/province?**

- **What is the animal like?**

Where did you find the information? _____

 Lesson 76 – Research Project
Gather Information– Topic #4

Your state/province: _____

Find at least two pictures that are connected to your fourth research topic. Attach the pictures to the spaces provided. Consider the research questions on the previous page to help guide you to find pictures. *Note: You will need two copies of each picture you choose: one to paste to this page and one to use in your final project.*

DO NOT USE PICTURES THAT ARE COPYRIGHTED.

A picture of an animal in
your state/province

A picture of a plant in your
state/province

Where did you find the information? _____

218

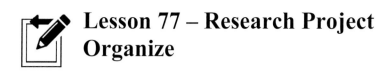

Lesson 77 – Research Project
Organize

The next step in the research process is to use the information that you gathered to organize your topic paragraphs.

Look at how the information is put into a graphic organizer:

Topic #3: Who is an important person from your state/province?

- *What is their name?* George HW Bush
- *When were they born?* 1924
- *What important thing did they do?* forty-first president

O	important person from Texas
D	name is George HW Bush
D	born in 1924
D	forty-first president → important
C	George HW Bush – important person from Texas

Look at how the graphic organizer is turned into a paragraph:

There is an important man from Texas. His name is George HW Bush. He was born in 1924. He was important because he was the forty-first president of the United States. Mr. Bush is an important person from Texas.

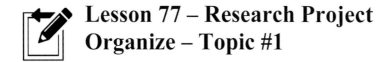

Lesson 77 – Research Project
Organize – Topic #1

Topic #1: What is your state/province?

Organize your first topic paragraph.

Use the graphic organizer to plan your
paragraph about your first topic.

Use the information you
gathered on page 211.

Opening	

Detail	

Detail	

Detail	

Closing	

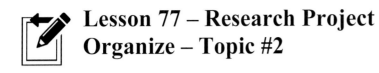

Lesson 77 – Research Project
Organize – Topic #2

Topic #2: What important event happened in your state/province?

Organize your second topic paragraph.

Use the graphic organizer to plan your paragraph about your second topic.

Use the information you gathered on page 213.

Opening >

Detail >

Detail >

Detail >

Closing >

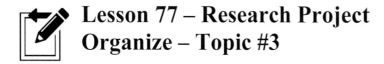

Lesson 77 – Research Project
Organize – Topic #3

Topic #3: Who is an important person from your state/province?

Organize your third topic paragraph.

Use the graphic organizer to plan your paragraph about your third topic.

Use the information you gathered on page 215.

Opening

Detail

Detail

Detail

Closing

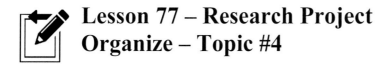

Lesson 77 – Research Project
Organize – Topic #4

Topic #4: What kinds of plants and animals are in your state/province?

Organize your fourth topic paragraph.

Use the graphic organizer to plan your paragraph about your fourth topic.

Use the information you gathered on page 217.

Opening

Detail

Detail

Detail

Closing

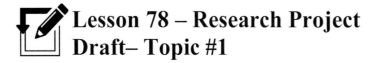

Lesson 78 – Research Project
Draft– Topic #1

Topic #1: What is your state/province?

Write your first topic paragraph on the lines below. Take the ideas from your plan on page 220 and make them complete sentences.

_____

_____

_____

_____

_____

_____

_____

_____

_____

_____

_____

_____

Lesson 78 – Research Project
Draft – Topic #2

Topic #2: What important event happened in your state/province?

Write your second topic paragraph on the lines below. Take the ideas from your plan on page 221 and make them complete sentences.

Lesson 78 – Research Project
Draft – Topic #3

Topic #3: Who is an important person from your state/province?

Write your third topic paragraph on the lines below. Take the ideas from your plan on page 222 and make them complete sentences.

_____

_____

_____

_____

_____

_____

_____

_____

_____

_____

_____

_____

_____

 **Lesson 78 – Research Project**
Draft– Topic #4

Topic #4: What kinds of plants and animals are in your state/province?

Write your fourth topic paragraph on the lines below. Take the ideas from your plan on **page 223** and make them complete sentences.

_____

_____

_____

_____

_____

_____

_____

_____

_____

_____

_____

_____

_____

Lesson 79 – Research Project
Revise

Look for ways to add descriptive adjectives and action verbs to your writing. If your sentences all begin with the same word, look for ways to use different beginning words.

Remember, you do not have to change *everything* you have written. Only make changes that ***improve*** your writing.

Draft
There is an important man from Texas.

Revised
Many important people are from Texas, but one stands out.

Revise your draft. Read your draft out loud, and touch each word as you read. Look for ways to add or change details, words, or sentences.

- Reading out loud will help you notice details you do not see when you read silently.
- Touching each word will help you focus on one thing at a time.

Read your draft out loud, and touch each word as you read. Revise each paragraph of your research project.

☐   **Revised words**

☐   **Revised sentences**

Lesson 80 – Research Project
Final Draft

Make **copies** of your revised drafts on new pieces of paper. **Edit** your writing to make sure capitalization, punctuation, and spelling are correct.

Copy each revised paragraph onto a clean sheet of notebook paper. Each paragraph should be on a separate sheet of paper.

Optional: Type each paragraph and print on separate sheets of paper.

Edit each paragraph. Check off each step as you complete it. (P = Paragraph)

Touch each word and read aloud. As you read, look for <u>capitalization</u> errors.

P #1   P #2   P #3   P #4

____   ____   ____   ____

Touch each word and read aloud. As you read, look for <u>punctuation</u> errors.

P #1   P #2   P #3   P #4

____   ____   ____   ____

Touch each word and read aloud. As you read, look for <u>spelling</u> errors.

P #1   P #2   P #3   P #4

____   ____   ____   ____

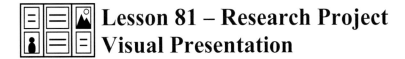 **Lesson 81 – Research Project**
Visual Presentation

To finish your research project, create a display board.

> ### SUPPLIES YOU WILL NEED
>
> - poster board
>
> - pencils, pens, or markers
>
> - letter stickers (optional)

Step #1 : Title

- **Add a title to the poster board. The title should be the name of your state/province.**

- **You can write the title or use stickers of letters to create the title.**

- **Put the title at the top and center of your poster board.**

Lesson 81 – Research Project
Visual Presentation

SUPPLIES YOU WILL NEED

- colored construction paper

- glue

- scissors

- the pictures you gathered during research

Step #2 : Pictures

- **Cut out the pictures you gathered during research.**

- **Glue the pictures onto colored pieces of construction paper.**

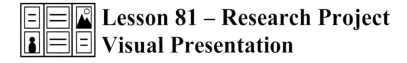

Lesson 81 – Research Project
Visual Presentation

SUPPLIES YOU WILL NEED

- colored construction paper

- glue

- scissors

- the final drafts of your topic paragraphs

Step #3 : Topic Paragraphs

- **Cut out the final drafts of your topic paragraphs.**

- **Glue the paragraphs onto colored pieces of construction paper.**

Lesson 81 – Research Project
Visual Presentation

SUPPLIES YOU WILL NEED

- glue
- the topic paragraphs on colored paper
- the pictures on colored paper

Step #4 : Arrange the Presentation

- **Arrange the pictures and paragraphs on your poster board.**

- **Glue the paragraphs and pictures onto the poster board.**

Lesson 81 – Research Project
Visual Presentation

SUPPLIES YOU WILL NEED

- glue

- pencils

- paper

- the names of the sources you used

Step #5 : Give Credit to the Sources You Used

- **Create your bibliography (see Lesson 82).**

- **Glue your bibliography to the back of your poster board.**

- **Write the following words on the bottom right corner of your poster board: *Bibliography on back.***

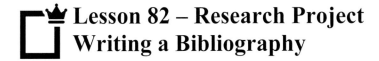

Lesson 82 – Research Project
Writing a Bibliography

A *bibliography* tells your reader where you got your information. It also gives credit to the authors of the sources you used.

Refer to the research you gathered in Lesson 76. Record where you got your information on a separate sheet of paper. Glue the sheet to the back of your poster board presentation.

Your bibliography should look something like this:

Bibliography

The State of Texas by Andre Alvarez

Famous People in the United States by Brenda Bekker

What's That Bird? by Chris Csonka

Interview with Deborah DiAngelo

Website: www.texas.gov

Research Project
Checklist

Process

☐ Did you follow the entire process as indicated in the lessons?

☐ Did you use your time wisely?

Written Paragraphs – Content

☐ Does each paragraph contain a quality opening sentence?

☐ Does each paragraph contain quality information about the state/province?

☐ Does each paragraph contain a quality closing sentence?

☐ Did you put the information in your own words and did not copy sentences directly from the sources?

Written Paragraphs – Mechanics

☐ Did you check your spelling?

☐ Did you use capitalization correctly?

☐ Did you use punctuation correctly?

☐ Did you indent the first sentence of each paragraph?

Visual Presentation

☐ Is your presentation neat and creative?

☐ Is your presentation organized and easy to read?

☐ Does your presentation have a title (state/province name)?

☐ Does your presentation include information about the sources you used?

Complete Unit Two
Comprehensive Assessment

Final Lesson – Comparing Compositions

Now that you have completed Level 3, it is time to see what you have learned.

Using the prompt below and what you have learned, write a composition. Remember to follow the writing process.

Pretend that you have just received a pen pal from a city far away. The pen pal wants to know what you are like. Describe two activities that you like to do.

_____

_____

_____

_____

_____

_____

_____

_____

_____

_____

_____

_____

After you finish, remove your first composition from the time capsule. Compare it to the one you have just written using the checklist on the next page.

Final Lesson – Comparing Compositions

Comparing the two compositions will help you see how far you have come. Keep any areas of improvement in mind as you transition to **Level 4**.

Use the following checklist to compare your compositions. The column labeled "#1" refers to your first composition, and "#2" refers to your last composition.

#1   #2

☐ ☐ **Did you follow the Writing Process?**

☐ ☐ **- Brainstorm**

☐ ☐ **- Organize**

☐ ☐ **- Draft**

☐ ☐ **- Revise**

☐ ☐ **- Final Draft**

Congratulations on becoming a better writer! I look forward to seeing you again next year!

☐ ☐ **Does your composition contain all parts?**

☐ ☐ **- A clear opening**

☐ ☐ **- Body sentences with clear details**

☐ ☐ **- A clear closing**

☐ ☐ **Did you communicate effectively?**

☐ ☐ **- Descriptive adjectives and action verbs**

☐ ☐ **- Not all sentences began the same way**

CONGRATULATIONS! YOU HAVE COMPLETED LEVEL 3.